CLASSICAL
KIMONO

FROM THE
KYOTO NATIONAL MUSEUM

Asian Art Museum of San Francisco

Kyoto National Museum

The Agency for Cultural Affairs

1997

Published by the Asian Art Museum of San Francisco
on the occasion of the exhibition
Four Centuries of Fashion: Classical Kimono from the Kyoto National Museum
February 5–March 23, 1997, jointly organized by the Asian Art Museum,
the Kyoto National Museum, and the Agency for Cultural Affairs

Distributed by University of Washington Press

Produced by Perpetua Press, Los Angeles
Production supervision for AAM by Michael Morrison
Edited by Michael Morrison and Lorna Price
Indexed by Yoko Woodson and Susan Coerr
Photography by Morio Kanai, Kyoto National Museum
Design by Dana Levy
Printed and bound in Hong Kong by C & C Offset Printing Co. Ltd. .

Library of Congress Cataloging-in-Publishing Data
ISBN 0-939117-09-6

The following objects courtesy of the Prince Takamatsu Collection:
cat. nos. 23 through 30.

The following objects courtesy of the Tamura Shizuko Collection:
cat. nos. 20, 21, 31, 32, 38, 47–50, 52–56, and 72–100.

Cover: *Kosode* for a Male Child with Horse-racing at Kamigamo Shrine, p. 61
pp. 1–3: *Kosode* with Flowing Streams and Chrysanthemums (detail), p. 51
p. 36: *Okuni Kabuki* (detail), pp. 42–43
p. 58: *Kosode* for a Male Child with Horse-racing at Kamigamo Shrine (detail), p. 61
p. 78: *Hosonaga* with Pine Lozenges and Light-blue Tortoise-shell Interlocking Pattern
(detail), p. 93
p. 98: *Koshimaki* with Myriad Treasures, Pine, Bamboo, and Plums (detail), p. 108
p. 112: Covered, Red-cornered Box with Yellow Roses and Flowering Water (detail), p. 116
p. 128: *Okuni Kabuki* (detail), pp. 42–43
Back cover: *Dōfuku* (samurai coat) with Paulwanias and Arrows, p. 39

THE ASIAN ART MUSUEM OF SAN FRANCISCO
is located in Golden Gate Park, San Francisco, CA 94118
Public information: 415-379-8879

Contents

Translation and adaptation by
Yoko Woodson and Richard Mellott

Foreword

THIS EXHIBITION is part of the exchange program established by Japan's Agency for Cultural Affairs. The program promotes understanding and friendship among the three national museums of Japan and foreign museums and galleries with acclaimed collections of arts that represent the culture of Asia.

In 1995, we were pleased to present the first part of the exchange, the exhibition *Oriental Art from the Asian Art Museum of San Francisco* at our museum. It included Buddhist arts from China, Japan, and Korea, together with a group of Chinese paintings and applied arts selected from some 12,000 objects in the museum's collections. The second part of our exchange, *Four Centuries of Fashion: Classical Kimono from the Kyoto National Museum*, is now presented by the Asian Art Museum of San Francisco.

From 794 on, Kyoto prospered; for more than a thousand years it was the *miyako*, where emperors resided. It was also the center for literature, art, and crafts, and particularly famous for leading Japan's fashion trends. Kyoto's *nishijin* weaving and *yūzen* dyeing produced beautifully decorated kimono. This exhibition focuses on the art of costume. It includes classical kimono, paintings depicting beauties and other people dressed in splendid robes, lacquered toiletry objects, and personal ornaments from the Momoyama and Edo periods. They illustrate how much the Japanese were concerned with attire and adornment. We hope this exhibition will help American people to understand the Japanese and their culture.

Finally, I wish to express our deep gratitude to the efforts of those who worked hard to realize this exhibition, and for the generosity of corporate donors.

NORIO FUJISAWA
Director, Kyoto National Museum
February, 1997

Foreword

THE CURRENT SUCCESS OF JAPANESE DESIGNERS in the world of international *haute couture* is a contemporary reflection of a long-standing love among the Japanese for clothing and fashion. The Asian Art Museum is very pleased to present an exhibition that documents the most glorious period of traditional textile arts. *Four Centuries of Fashion: Classical Kimono from the Kyoto National Museum Collection* traces that interest prior to the modern age.

The Asian Art Museum deeply appreciates the opportunity to participate in an exchange agreement that was established between the two museums as part of a program initiated in 1993 by the Agency for Cultural Affairs in Tokyo. In the autumn of 1995, for the first part of the exchange, the Asian Art Museum took an exhibition of Chinese paintings and objects and Japanese Buddhist paintings and objects from our collections to Kyoto. Now our colleagues in Kyoto have assembled 100 works of classical kimono, or *kosode*, accessories, toilet articles, and paintings. All are beautifully selected to show the development of Japan's textile manufacture and design as well as changing fashion trends from the sixteenth to the nineteenth centuries.

On behalf of the commissioners and Trustees of the Asian ArtMuseum, we wish to express our great thanks to the Agency for Cultural Affairs for its generous support of the project, and to the Director, Mr. Norio Fujisawa, the Chief Curator, Mr. Masahiko Kawahara, and staff of the Kyoto National Museum for the many efforts and the friendly cooperation that brought the exhibition to fruition.

This exhibition catalogue is an excellent collaboration among scholars from both museums. Mr. Hiroyuki Kano, Curator of Japanese Paintings, Mr. Akio Haino, Curator of Lacquerware, and Shigeki Kawakami, Curator of Textiles wrote catalogue entries. Mr. Kawakami's text, together with an essay by Dr. Yoko Woodson, Curator of Japanese Art of the Asian Art Museum, and numerous illustrations make this volume an important contribution to the literature in English on Japanese dress. The Japanese writings were translated by Dr. Woodson with the assistance of Richard Mellott.

The catalogue was edited by Michael Morrison and Lorna Price, and the handsome design is a credit to the skills of Dana Levy of Perpetua Press. To all these individuals we extend congratulations and thanks for their accomplishments and dedicated commitment to excellence

EMILY J. SANO,
Director, Asian Art Museum of San Francisco
February, 1997

The Asian Art Museum is grateful for the generous support
of the following institutions for this exhibition and catalogue

E. RHODES AND LEONA B. CARPENTER FOUNDATION

THE SOCIETY FOR ASIAN ART

THE COMMEMORATIVE ASSOCIATION
FOR THE JAPAN WORLD EXPOSITION (1970)

SHAKLEE CORPORATION

And acknowledges the ongoing programmatic support of

THE HARRY G. C. PACKARD COLLECTION
CHARITABLE TRUST FOR FAR EASTERN ART STUDIES

FORMING
THE NATIONAL STYLE

CLASSICAL KIMONO IN
HISTORICAL REVIEW

Yoko Woodson

THE GARMENTS, UTENSILS, AND PERSONAL objects in this exhibition were made for everyday use. They eloquently illustrate everyday use. They eloquently illustrate the life of the Japanese people during the entire span of the Momoyama (1573–1615) and Edo (1615–1867) periods. During these four centuries, Japanese culture and art matured thoroughly to form the indigenous Japanese style in all expressions of art. Selected from the acclaimed collections of the Kyoto National Museum, each object represents the best of its kind. Two of the paintings and three *kosode* are designated Important Cultural Properties.

The *kosode* above all blossomed in this period, when textile production reached its highest level of accomplishment in weaving technique and design. The Japanese pursued perfection in their weaving, but at the same time they became less dependent on weaving techniques for the decoration of their robes. Because the sumptuous woven textiles required extensive labor and artisans' time, consumers turned to dyeing, which could produce decorated fabrics of equal beauty at less expense. In addition, though the woven silks of earlier periods greatly enriched the robes, the voluminous fabric was stiff and cumbersome. The decorative motifs woven into these fabrics were geometrically composed, with mechanical regularity. Though they were beautiful and harmonious, the designs achieved by this method are not completely satisfying for the Japanese, because they have no metaphorical or allusive meaning. The Japanese loved nature, which inspired every detail of their lives. They longed for beautiful, natural, and meaningful decoration in their garments, and explored the utmost possibilities of dyeing for this end. In contrast to weaving, dyework allowed a free and graphic style that used myriad motifs in bold compositions. By the middle of the seventeenth century, the Japanese had developed splendid dyeworks that impressed a foreign visitor, João Rodrigues, the Portuguese interpreter, who commented:

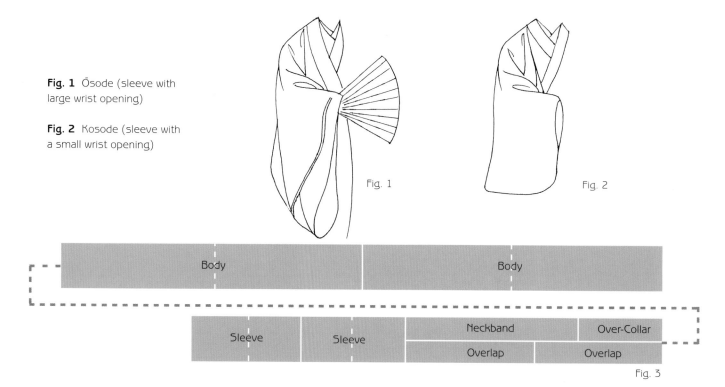

Fig. 1 Ōsode (sleeve with large wrist opening)

Fig. 2 Kosode (sleeve with a small wrist opening)

Fig. 1

Fig. 2

Body

Body

Sleeve

Sleeve

Neckband

Over-Collar

Overlap

Overlap

Fig. 3

Fig. 3 Cut of the fabric of kosode of later period and contemporary kimono. Woven width of cloth 36 cm Overall length of fabric approx. 1,100 cm Body length 140 cm Sleeve length 51 cm Overlap length 120 cm

And the Japanese are extremely skillful in this matter of dyeing their robes of silk and other cloth, they intermingled gold among the flowers painted in diverse way, and they are especially clever in their use of crimson and, even more, of violet. [1]

The development of dyeing techniques accelerated remarkably toward the end of the seventeenth century. *Yūzen* dyeing, a complex technique combining paste-resist dyeing and painting, made it possible to dye a fabric with a complicated design. Old and new woven patterns—small floral rondels, tortoise-shell grid, and key fret—were integrated in monochrome figures into the backgrounds of the dyed decorative compositions. Sometimes embroidery and application of metallic foils on fabric (*surihaku*) enriched the designs—a tendency already begun in the Muromachi period (1392–1573).

In the largest sense of its meaning, the word "kimono" means clothing (lit. things to wear). In the twentieth century it means Japanese-style clothing, in contrast to Western-style dress. The beautiful kimono, with its straight cut and sewing, is acknowledged as Japan's unique indigenous costume.

Ōsode and Kosode

TWO SLEEVE TYPES differentiate the basic Japanese style of robes. *Ōsode* (lit. large sleeve), the older type, has large, loose sleeves with a wide wrist opening the entire width of the sleeve (fig. 1). This type of sleeve allowed the wearers a layered look so that the sleeve edge of the garment underneath peeked out from beneath the edge of the top garment's sleeve. Made with stiff, woven-silk fabrics, voluminous *ōsode* are generally associated with the costume of the court nobles and ladies. They are still in use in the imperial court for ceremonies and theatrical performances such as *bugaku* (masked dance) and Noh dramas.

The *kosode* has sleeves with a small wrist opening (fig. 2). It was originally worn under *ōsode* robes as an undergarment. The term *kosode* is applied even to robes with

Fig. 4 *Kosode* from around 1600.

Fig. 5 Kimono, front.

Fig. 6 Kimono, back.

long swinging sleeves (*furisode*) if they have small wrist openings. *Kosode* as undergarments were made of simpler materials, such as ramie and plain-weave silks. They were gradually decorated, at first simply and later more elaborately. When it attained the status of an outer garment, the *kosode* was made with more elaborate materials, such as silk twills (*aya-ori*), figured satin (*rinzu*), and crepes (*chirimen*), which were soft and suitable for dyed decorations and embroidery.

Kosode (and later kimono) are ankle-length, one-piece robes. Unlike Western garments, they have no curves at armholes and upper sleeves, no darts, no gathers, no tacks or gored panels. This concept of a straight-cut and flat garment to enclose the body continued unchanged up to the twentieth century. The construction of the *kosode* is simple. A bolt of cloth is cut only across its width into seven straight pieces: two long body panels, two sleeves, two overlaps, and a neckband (fig. 3). Earlier *kosode* were wider, but became narrower: in the late sixteenth century, the woven cloth panel was approximately 45 cm wide (fig. 4), whereas in the modern kimono it is 36 cm wide. The body panels are sewn at the center back and sides. To each front panel is added an overlap. To this body, sleeves and a long neckband are attached (figs. 5, 6).

In making *kosode* and kimono, nothing is wasted. To adjust it to different body sizes, the width of the fabric is taken in at the sides, and the excess material remains uncut as a wide seam. In the twentieth century, the fabric of an existing kimono, unless it is embroidered, is customarily bleached and redyed with an entirely new design. For example, a middle-aged woman's youthful-looking kimono may be redyed with a more subdued design suitable for her age, or a mother's kimono can be redesigned for her young daughter. If the materials are worn out, the sound portions can be reused for *futon* covers, cushions, and smaller objects.

The cut and stitching of *kosode* were standardized, for they were worn by both men and women as well as young and old of all classes and positions. They were also

distinguished individual uses and tastes. On the flattened, T-shaped space of the *kosode*, ingenious designers tried to meet their customers' very diverse demands. Drawing their images from nature, literature, legends, and everyday life, *kosode* designers could turn any subject to their decorative motifs. Their ambitious pursuits were challenged by this enormous task of individualizing the standardized cut and stitching (fig. 7).

Evolution of *Kosode*

THE *KOSODE* PROSPERED for over 400 years, and its basic form continued as the kimono. However, the evolution of the *kosode* took a long time. From prehistoric times, when a crude cloth simply covered a human body, until the *kosode* style came to maturity, the Japanese costume underwent major changes, sometimes accepting foreign influences and digesting and assimilating them to native uses and taste.

The earliest accounts of Japanese clothing occur in a Chinese historical document of the third century, the *Weizhi weiren zhuan*, or Wei Chronicle. The subsection *Dongyi zhuan* (Eastern Barbarian Accounts) mentions:

> Men wear covered their hair with a cloth of hemp (*asa*). They also cover their bodies with a horizontal cloth, which is not sewn. Women tie and fold their hair. They wear an unlined cloth with a central hole through which they put their heads.[2]

It seems that in ancient times, Japanese men wore a cloth wrapped around their body like a sarong and the women wore a cloth like a poncho.

During the Yayoi period (250 BC–AD 250), when the *Weizhi* was compiled, the Japanese developed agriculture and settled in communities. Their Chinese counterparts, however, had enjoyed a far more developed civilization; their clothing, for example, had sleeves and a neckband. It is possible that the Chinese influence had either not reached Japan or had not yet brought enough impact on Japanese costume.

Fig. 8

Fig. 9

Visual evidence on clothing abounds in the subsequent Kofun period (Old Tombs; 250–552) in the many clay figures called *haniwa*. These figures ornament the tops of the cylindrical clay posts that reinforced the gigantic tomb-mounds constructed for powerful figures of the time. Of simple sculptural form, *haniwa* represent humans, animals, horses, boats, and houses, illustrating prehistoric Japanese life. A warrior *haniwa* (fig. 8) wears a three-quarter length tunic with narrow half-sleeves and voluminous trousers that are tied below the knee, making them billow around the upper leg. A separate belt completes this costume.

A *haniwa* woman (fig. 9) wears a similar tunic with a front flap fastened across at the left side, and a skirt that appears to be pleated. Her hair is tied into a chignon at the top of the head. The clothes of both *haniwa* show a simple style of tailoring. In this period, cloth or leather was cut to fit three-dimensional bodies, and anatomical differences in men and women were taken into account.

The materials used for clothing in this period were leather, and the bark of trees such as mulberry, vines, and hemp. Silk fabrics were already in use, as the *Weizhi* remarks on the existence of sericulture in Japan[3]. The fabrics were dyed in several colors with dyestuffs taken from plants—red from *akane* (madder), blue from *yamaai* (indigo from buckwheat), yellow from *kariyasu* (miscanthus), and purple from *murasaki* (gromwell root).[4]

The Japanese historical period began in 552, with the transmission of Buddhism from India via China and Korea. It inaugurated a golden age of Buddhism and the related culture of the Asuka (552–710) and Nara (710–794) periods. By this time Japan was consolidated under the Yamato court, the origin of Japan's imperial rule which has lasted to the present day. After some political disputes, Buddhism was accepted as the national religion; closer contacts with China and its continent then brought a wide range of Chinese and continental influences to the isolated island country.

In 603, Emperor Suiko adopted the dress code of the Sui court and established the rules of crowns (*kanmuri*) for court nobles, the *Twelve Ranks of the Crowns*.[5] The code, curiously, did not regulate clothing. It is likely that nobles' robes had been already developed, and therefore it was not necessary to mention costume. The eighth-century chronicle *Nihon shoki*, however, says that men wore a short, pleated decorative panel (*mo* or *hirami*) over their trousers.[6]

A Chinese chronicle, the *Suishu* of the Sui dynasty, mentions that women wore a pleated decoration (*hirami*) and pleated skirt (*mo*). The Tenjukoku Mandala, an embroidery illustrating imaginary scenes of the Buddhist heaven, made in 622 by Tachibana no Ōiratsume in memory of her late husband Prince Shōtoku, offers a confirmation of this Chinese description. In this mandala, women wear a tunic with a round neck and narrow sleeves with a wide cuff, a horizontal decorative border, and pleated *hirami* around the hem (fig. 10), under which they wear a pleated skirt. They carry a bag on a strap that goes from the right shoulder to left; its function is unknown.

In the eighth century, textile industries were organized more formally under government sponsorship. Until this time, weaving had remained a hereditary industry. Now anyone was free to enter the business and work under the supervision of the Ministry of the Treasury.[7]

Fig. 10 Women. Tenjukoku Mandala (detail), embroidery. Dated 622. Chūgūji, Nara prefecture. *Asuka Hakuhō no bijutsu, Nihon bijutsu zenshū,* vol. 3, 1980, pl. 22. Photo: Gakushū Kenkyūsha, Tokyo.

Fig. 11 Ladies in procession. Painting on west wall of Takamatsu-zuka tomb, Asuka-mura, Nara (detail). Second half of 7th century. *Asuka Hakuhō no bijutsu, Nihon bijutsu zenshū,* vol. 3, pl. 8, 1980. Photo: Gakushū Kenkyūsha, Tokyo.

Fig. 10   Fig. 11

Paintings in the Takamatsu-zuka tomb in Nara further enrich the visual sources on women and men of the time. These paintings, discovered in 1972 in a small unpretentious tomb, are dated to the second half of the seventh century. A painting on the west wall illustrates a procession of a group of women (fig. 11). Their tunics with long sleeves and a wide cuff, and striped skirts with pleated *mo* resemble those in the Tenjukoku Mandala. One difference is that the tunics in the Takamatsu-zuka have a neckband that closes in a V-shape in front, and the right body panel covers the left one. A ribbon and a belt in the same or a different color decorate the neckband and the lower tunic respectively. The figure type changed from slender, in the Tenjukoku Mandala, to a plump type, revealing that the Japanese had adopted the plump woman of the Tang dynasty as the ideal.

A fully matured international phase of Buddhism occurred in the subsequent Nara period. Government sponsored Buddhism built many Buddhist temples and furnished them with many sculptures. The treasures in the Shōsō-in, the imperial storehouse located in the precinct of the Tōdaiji temple in Nara, illustrate Japanese court life heavily under the influence of the aristocratic life of Tang China. The treasures of Emperor Shōmu's court were presented to Tōdaiji by his wife, Empress Kōmyō, after his death in 756. Some of the treasures were clearly made in China, and some others are identified as being of Japanese origin.

The painting *Standing Beauties under Trees*, a six-panel screen, portrays in each panel a beauty either standing or seated. The plump women with coiffure and make-up including beauty spots on their foreheads add another example of the ideal beauty of Tang China (fig. 12). Listed as the "Screen of Ladies with Birds' Feathers," the figures were once covered with feathers except for their flesh, faces and hands. Now the feathers are all gone, and the panels reveal the underdrawing. The lady wears a thin, flowing robe with a round neck; it is tied with a long ribbon at the center and has narrow sleeves.

Fig. 12 *Standing Beauty under a Tree.* Six-fold screen (detail). Mid-8th century. Imperial Collection of the Shō sō-in, Nara. *Shōsō-in no kaiga shoseki, Nihon bijutsu zenshū*, vol. 5, 1980, pl. 81. Photo: Gakushū kenkyūsha, Tokyo.

Fig. 13 Fujiwara no Michinaga, *Murasaki Shikibu nikki emaki* handscroll (detail). 13th century. Gotō Museum Collection, Tokyo. *Genshoku Nihon no bijutsu*, vol. 8, 1968, pl. 59. Photo: Shōgakukan, Tokyo.

Fig. 12

Fig. 13

A piece of paper used for reinforcing the screen was discovered to be an administrative archive paper bearing the Japanese date 752,[8] proving this screen was made in Japan. The lady's costume shows some changes compared with the tunic-type robe in the Tenjukoku Mandala and in the wall painting of the Takamatsu-zuka tomb. The two-piece dress with tunic and skirt became a long, one-piece dress, obviously made of thin fabric.

Emergence of a Japanese Style

AFTER A FEW PROSPEROUS CENTURIES, Japan went into stagnation, and corruption developed in the government and the Buddhist establishment. To reform the government and to avoid interference by the Buddhist monks, in 794 the capital was moved from Nara to Heian-kyō (capital of peace and tranquility; present-day Kyoto) some thirty miles away from Nara.

In China, the once strong and powerful Tang dynasty grew increasingly weaker until 907, when it finally fell. Its influence over neighboring countries had already been waning. In 894, Japan terminated its relations with China, ceasing to send its diplomatic mission there. Japan began a long phase of contemplating its own affairs. The court nobles and ladies cultivated their tastes in art and literature. They were excessively concerned with manners and etiquette, and lavished a great love on costume. In order to support their large, extravagant, and expensive wardrobes, large quantities of silk were produced under imperial supervision at the Imperial Weaving Bureau, which was installed in the city of Kyoto.[9] Subsequently the silk industry spread all over the country. At the same time, an enormous amount of silk was continuously imported from China.

By the mid-Heian period, the distinctive court style had gradually evolved, characterized by rich woven materials and grand forms. Both men's and women's robes had square-cut and enormously large sleeves. Semiformal dress for courtiers consisted of the *nōshi*, a double-breasted robe with large sleeves, a round neckline with a standing band fastened on the right shoulder, and *sashinuki* trousers (*hakama*), pleated trousers

Fig. 14

with a drawstring at the ankle, which caused the bottoms of the trousers to form balloonlike puffs (fig. 13). The colors of their semiformal robes were not prescribed by their rank in court society.

The fully developed formal costume for court ladies was a layered look, "twelve layered robes" (*jūnihitoe*), as it was termed by the people of later periods (fig. 14). It consisted of a short cloak (*karaginu*), outer garment (*uwagi*), a lined garment (*uchiginu*), a set of layered robes in different colors (*uchiki*), an unlined garment (*hitoe*), a divided skirt (*hakama*), and a long, pleated panel *(mo)*. The *uchiki* was a key to composing the costume in "twelve layers of garments." They were made of plain silks, in colors carefully chosen to harmonize; these colored layers were revealed at the neck, at the front edges, and at the wide openings of the *ōsode*. Nobles and their ladies, engulfed by their beautiful, stiff, silk garments, were frequently portrayed in the paintings of the Heian (794–1185) and Kamakura (1185–1333) periods.

Clothing of Working People

WORKING PEOPLE OF ALL PERIODS wore much simpler clothes than courtiers. Under no necessity to demonstrate their power and social status by their garments, they maintained an honest, rational attitude toward costume. Their concern was for the functionality, comfort, and affordability of their clothes. The background painting to the Lotus Sutra on a fan-shaped paper (fig. 15) depicts a washerwoman putting up a thin, unlined blue *hitoe* to dry on a clothes-rod near a well. The garment may belong to her mistress, who is seated at the left. The washerwoman wears a short, indigo tie-dyed, sleeveless summer garment (*tenashi*, without sleeves) over a white wrapped skirt, and wooden clogs. This healthy, comfortable-looking woman contrasts with her moody young mistress, who seems overwhelmed by her *jūnihitoe* on one of Kyoto's notoriously hot, humid summer days.

Working people had been wearing *kosode* as an outer garment. Around the twelfth century, men and women of the nobility began to wear it as an undergarment next to the

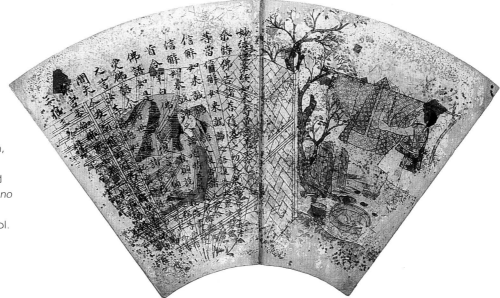

Fig. 15

skin. Greatly concerned with etiquette, they seldom revealed it. A scene from the famous handscroll *Ban Dainagon ekotoba* (Story of Ban, Secretary of State), illustrates ladies in the Minamoto no Makoto's house in violent gestures of grief on learning that their master was falsely blamed for having set fire to the main gate of the imperial palace. The weeping ladies, momentarily abandoning etiquette, here reveal their *kosode* (fig. 16)—a way that the artist has chosen to graphically convey the depth of their anguish.

Emergence of *Kosode*

THE COURT ARISTOCRATS discovered the comfort of wearing *kosode* as underwear, but they took a long time to discard their cumbersome outer garments. It required a rational attitude on the wearers' part as well as artistic and technical developments on the designers' part in order to make *kosode* into beautiful outer garments.

While the court aristocrats leisurely indulged in art, literature, and fashion, imperial power was slowly slipping into the hands of warrior leagues (*bushi dan*) in the provinces. These warriors were entrusted to maintain order in the nobles' and temples' estates in the countryside. By the mid and late Heian periods, the powerful warrior (*samurai*) clans began to exert control over the court. Among the larger warrior leagues were the Taira and Minamoto clans. They struggled with each other for supreme power, engaging in a series of wars. The winner, Minamoto Yoritomo, became the first shogun in Japan's history and established the *bakufu* (military government) in Kamakura, northeastern Japan. Thus began four periods of shogunal government (*bakufu* or shogunate) during the Kamakura, Muromachi (1392–1573), Momoyama (1573–1615), and Edo periods. The capital moved from Kamakura to Kyoto in the Muromachi period, and then to Edo in the Edo period. The imperial court still existed in Kyoto and the emperors and courtiers still devoted themselves to rituals and literature, but they had become impoverished.

The warriors maintained their martial heritage, their rational, practical outlook, and they engaged in physical activities. Although they modeled their formal robes for

Fig. 16 Grieving women in Minamoto no Makoto's house. The women grieve because their master was falsely blamed for setting fire to the main gate of the imperial palace. *Ban Dainagon ekotoba* (detail). 12th century. *Ban Dainagon ekotoba, Nihon emaki zenshū*, v. IV. Photo: Kadokawa Shoten, Tokyo.

Fig. 17 Court ladies in white *kosode* and trailing red *hakama* trousers (detail). *Ōeyama emaki*, Muromachi period, Tokyo National Museum. *History of Japanese Costume*, pl. 9. Photo: Charles Tuttle Co., Tokyo.

Fig. 16 Fig. 17

official functions and ceremonies after imperial garments, they preferred simple clothing and adopted the *kosode* as an informal outer garment. Women of the samurai class tended not to wear the formal *hakama* and wore an ankle-length *kosode* instead. *Kosode* originally made with ramié and plain-weave silk were now made with figured silks. During the civil wars, the deprived nobles obliged themselves to adopt simpler garments. Court ladies wore *kosode* and *hakama* as everyday clothes (fig. 17), keeping their traditional costumes for ceremonial occasions.

It was pertinent to beautify the *kosode* and its accessory, the sash (*obi*). *Obi* were still narrow, but were made with beautiful fabrics and cords. The most effective technique for decorating *kosode* was dyeing. During the Nara period, three dyeing techniques were used: clamp-resist dyeing, wax-resist dyeing, and tie-resist dyeing. Examples of all of these exist in the Shōsō-in storehouse. They were, however, overshadowed by intricate weaving techniques, and only tie-dyeing techniques were used continuously.[10] The artistic potential of this technique was realized in the late sixteenth century, when it blossomed in *tsujigahana* and the tiny-pattern tie dyeing called *kanoko shibori*. In the Momoyama period, beautifully decorated *kosode* became available (fig. 18).

Triumph of the Japanese Style

A COMPLEX PALETTE became an important key to achieving beautiful *kosode* designs. Obtaining dyestuffs required knowledge and experience in finding and expanding dye sources, extracting pigments, and then dyeing the fabrics and yarns and fixing the colors with mordants. During the Edo period, the Japanese palette for *kosode* expanded remarkably. The basic colors were reds and purples, blues, greens, yellows, browns, grays, and black (see appendix), which created myriad color variations.

Three main sources of red were madder (*akane*) root, safflower (*benibana*) petals, and sappanwood (*suō*) chips. A deep maroon-crimson (*enji*) is derived from the lac insect. Sappanwood chips and lac-based *enji* were imported from India through Dutch traders.

Fig. 18 Dancing woman in *kosode* (detail). Hanging scroll, Momoyama period. *100 Masterpieces from the Collection of the Suntory Museum of Art*, 1981, pl. 21. Photo: Suntory Museum of Art, Tokyo.

Fig. 18

Purple, an elegant color long monopolized by the shogunal family and Buddhist clergy of the highest rank, was extracted from *murasaki* (gromwell) roots. A variant of this color, *nise murasaki* (resembling purple) was obtained in a dual process; indigo was first used for dark blue, and then *suō* was applied on top of it.

Blue, the favorite color of all times, was used without restriction by all classes. It was obtained from indigo, which was readily cultivated in Japan. Indigo dye produces blue ranging from pale to the darkest of hues. It was also an important base color for obtaining other colors, including black. Green is obtained by top-dyeing yellow and indigo. The sources of yellows are *kihada* (philodendron), *kuchinashi* (gardenia), *enju* (*Sophora japonica*), and *ukon* (turmeric). Yellow was also an important ingredient for obtaining browns.

Browns and grays could be used without restriction by commoners. Though subdued and somber, they fulfilled the aesthetic of the tea ceremony, and thus their subtle range of hues gained status, creating a new dimension of Japanese style. Tannin, the chemical component that produced both brown and gray, was obtained from various woods. Mordanted with elemental iron and alkali, tannin produces gray and brown respectively. Black, austere but later considered appropriate for formal wear, was obtained by top-dyeing indigo and madder. Another method was to top-dye *sumi* (ink) over indigo. In the second half of the nineteeth century, logwood, of Mexican and South American origin, became popular.

Kosode designs from the sixteenth to the nineteenth century embody the best of the Japanese decorative style in a balance of opposites: expressive but not sentimental; filling the ground or space but not overcrowding it; delicate but not weak; bold but not rough; bright but not gaudy; perfect spatial balance but not a rigid symmetry. The achievement of the Japanese style in *kosode* designs contains the synthesis of artistic and technical accomplishments in weaving, dyeing, and embroidery, incorporating decorative designs derived from long traditions of painting and crafts executed through the sophisticated use of dyestuffs.

NOTES

1. S. J. Michael Cooper, ed., *They Came to Japan; an Anthology of European Reports on Japan 1543–1640* (Berkeley: University of California Press, 1965), p. 206.

2. *Weizhi weiren zhuan* (Records of the Wei Kingdom: An Account of the Japanese), subsection *Dongyi zhuan* (The Eastern Barbarians), in Tsunoda and Goodrich, *Japan in the Chinese Dynastic Histories* (New York: Perkins Asiatic Monographs no. 2, 1951), p. 8–16; also quoted in Gafū Izutsu, *Nihon josei fukusōshi* (Kyoto: Kōrinsha, 1986), p. 16.

3. Quoted in James Ulak, *Five Centuries of Japanese Kimono* (Chicago: The Art Institute of Chicago, 1992), p. 73.

4. Gafū Izutsu, *Genshoku Nihon fukoshokushi* (Kyoto: Kōrinsha, 1982), p. 284.

5. *Ibid.*

6. Gafū Izutsu, *Nihon josei fukushokushi*, p. 23.

7. Helen Benton Minnich, *Japanese Costume and the Makers of Elegant Traditon* (Tokyo: Charles E. Tuttle Co., 1963), p. 64.

8. Shirō Gotō, ed., *Shōsō-in, Nihon bijutsu zenshū*, vol. 5 (Tokyo: Gakushū Kenkyūsha, 1978), p. 171.

9. Minnich, *Japanese Costume*, p. 107.

10. Yoshiko Wada et al., *Shibori; The Inventive Art of Japanese Shaped Resist Dyeing—Tradition, Techniques, Innovation* (Tokyo: Kōdansha, 1983), p. 15.

Clad in
Beautiful Colors
and
Myriad Motifs

Shigeki Kawakami

IN JAPAN'S LONG HISTORY OF COSTUME DESIGN, the Momoyama (1573–1615) and Edo (1615–1868) periods are characterized by gorgeous *kosode* worn by both men and women, young and old alike. *Kosode* are the predecessors of kimono, which are considered Japan's indigenous costume.

Until the mid-nineteenth century, one-piece robes with long sleeves and small wrist openings were called *kosode* (lit. small sleeve). Their origin goes back to the Heian period (794–1185), when court nobles wore them beneath outer robes. During the subsequent Muromachi (1392–1573) and Momoyama periods, *kosode* were decorated and came into use as outer garments. However, only in the Edo period did *kosode* achieve their highest artistic level, being decorated with designs that progressed hand-in-hand with newly developing dyeing techniques. During the Edo period, catalogues of *kosode* designs, equivalent to modern fashion magazines, were published in quantity. Curiously, the illustrations in these catalogues presented *kosode* designs only on the back of the garment. The designers' attention seemed to focus solely on this area to the exclusion of the front panels.

The designers showed no interest in changing the shape of *kosode* by cutting or adding elements to them. They seem to have considered the angular *kosode* shape—two long panels that cover the front and back of the body, and the two sleeves—as the only one suitable to enclose a human body. This outlook contrasts sharply with Western dress designs, in which the cut and shape of the garments are the designers' main concerns. The shape of *kosode*, made by straight cuts and stitching, continued unchanged for the following four centuries. Thus the decorative composition was the only area in which the designers were able to display any creativity.

The beauty of *kosode* is enhanced by the personality and movements of the wearer. Yet *kosode* can be appreciated for their designs on a flat surface, as shown in the fashion books. For example, sometimes on picnics people would take several *kosode* and hang them on a rope stretched between two trees. The picnickers enjoyed their robes suspended in the air as *kosode maku* (*kosode* drapes). On *kosode*, the designers' artistic talents and the wearers' aesthetic tastes were expressed through the decorative designs.

Tsujigahana DURING THE MUROMACHI and Momoyama periods, when *kosode* began to be used as outer garments, appropriate decorative designs for these new garments were explored. Colors and motifs were enclosed in contrasting zones, such as *katamigawari* (vertical right and left halves of the body) and *dangawari* (alternating horizontal bands or checkerboards).

Previously the decoration of robes relied on woven patterns. These patterns were, however, restrictive and repetitive. As designers of *kosode* wished to create more dynamic designs, they came to rely on the flexible techniques of dyeing and embroidery. *Tsujigahana* (lit. crossroad flowers; the term is etymologically obscure), a new dyeing technique, was created out of necessity during this period, and the *kosode* designs reflected the aesthetic and techniques of the period at their best.

The basic technique of *tsujigahana* is stitch-resist (*nuishime*) tie-dyeing. Before dyeing, motifs are outlined with running stitches, which are pulled tight and then wound closely with thread to prevent the penetration of dye. This produces patterns in reserve. The purpose of this tie-dyeing is not to create the interesting textures of tiny tie-dyeing called *kanoko shibori* (lit. "fawn spot"), but to create patterns in reserve. During the early phase of *tsujigahana*-dyeing development, it was easier to reserve smaller areas in white against a colored ground. Subsequent technical advances, however, made it possible to create more complex designs in multicolored divisions against a white ground. *Tsujigahana* is considered to have reached its maturity during the Tenshō era (1573–1592) of the Momoyama period.

Around this time, *tsujigahana* was widely used to decorate not only *kosode* but also *dōfuku*, the short jackets worn by samurai generals over their armor on the battlefield, or over *kosode* at home for relaxation. Some *dōfuku* were boldly decorated with *tsujigahana*. For example, two *tsujigahana*-decorated *dōfuku* with distinguished provenances show this dyeing technique at its highest level. One *dōfuku* is said to have been used by Toyotomi Hideyoshi (1537–1598; cat. no. 1) and the other by Tokugawa Ieyasu (1542–1616). These two men fought for national leadership in an attempt to consolidate war-torn Japan; the brilliant strategist Hideyoshi fell ill and died in disappointment, and Ieyasu succeeded in unifying the country, becoming the first shogun of the Tokugawa Bakufu (military government).

Tsujigahana-decorated robes were very likely supplied by dry-goods shops. Ledgers of custom-dyed robes in 1602 at the Kariganeya, a famous dry-goods store in Kyoto, recorded a *dōfuku* with *tsujigahana* designs which sounds very much like the one commissioned by Ieyasu. The store's ledgers also recorded commissions by nearly 200 other customers, including the second shogun Tokugawa Hidetada (1579–1632) and his wife, as well as Hideyoshi's wife Kita no Mandokoro Nene (1548–1624). These records suggest that *tsujigahana* continued to be in fashion among the upper class through the late sixteenth and into the early seventeenth centuries.

Nuihaku   TWO OTHER DECORATIVE TECHNIQUES popularly used during the Momoyama period were embroidery and gold and silver foil application (*nuihaku*). Bernardino de Avila Giron, a Spanish merchant, wrote in his book, *Relación del Reino de Nippon a que Llaman Corruptamente Jappon* (Account of the Kingdom of Nippon, Vulgarly Called Japan): "*Kimono*…[that is], clothes that the Japanese wear, are truly splendid. *Kimono* in good quality are beautifully dyed on silk ground, embellished further with gold foil and embroidery." The kimonos he observed were obviously gorgeously decorated with embroidery and gold foil. Unlike woven patterns, embroidery has great flexibility and can vary in the color, shape, or size of the designs; it was far superior, in terms of flexibility, for decorating robes. Gold and silver foils further enriched these decorations. During the Momoyama period, the embroidery was executed first, then filled in with metal foil between the motifs, adding a rich, sumptuous effect. The embroidery of this period is characterized by the soft finish of long floating stitches (*watashi nui*) done with untwisted silk floss. The motifs are defined clearly and simply, but with less concern for realistic depictions.

Kosode Designs of Four Seasons   *KOSODE,* WORN AS OUTER ROBES during the Muromachi period, were decorated in the tradition of the Heian period; they were each embellished with motifs of one of the seasons. From the end of the Muromachi to the Momoyama period, *kosode* began to be decorated with flowers with no seasonal differentiations. The *kosode* design (cat. no. 2) consisted of four blocks that might include four seasonal motifs: plum blossoms of spring, wisteria of summer, maples of autumn; and snow-covered bamboo of winter. The block of maples in vermilion tones on the right shoulder matches the spring plums in a similar tone at the left hem, and the block of green, snow-covered bamboo on the left shoulder matches well the wisterias of summer on the right hem. Other seasonal motifs of the Momoyama period included cherry blossoms, horsetails, dandelions, and violets of spring; irises of summer; chrysanthemums, maples, bush clovers, and pampas grass of autumn; and reeds and willows of winter. Other favorite motifs such as turtle shells were taken from the ocean beaches.

Keichō-Style Kosode   THE DECORATION of *kosode* with *tsujigahana* and *nuihaku,* two widely used decorative techniques, blossomed during the Momoyama period but fell out of fashion in the subsequent Keichō era (1596–1614). They were then revived as a new technique combining both. These *kosode* looked entirely different and came to be identified as Keichō-style *kosode* by scholars of Japanese textiles.

During the Momoyama period, *kosode* were often designed by placing decorative motifs in clearly defined zones: shoulder and hem areas (*kata suso*; fig. 1), alternating horizontal bands or blocks (*dangawari*; fig. 2), or vertical right and left halves of the body (*katamigawari*; fig. 3). These traditional decorative compositions derived from the medieval period. Keichō *kosode,* however, broke these divisions and created unified, dynamic compositions (fig. 4). The ground was dyed by *somewake,* tie-dyeing in complex interlocking shapes in black, red, and white, which were further decorated with fine motifs such as flowers executed in embroidery, and with small metal-foil

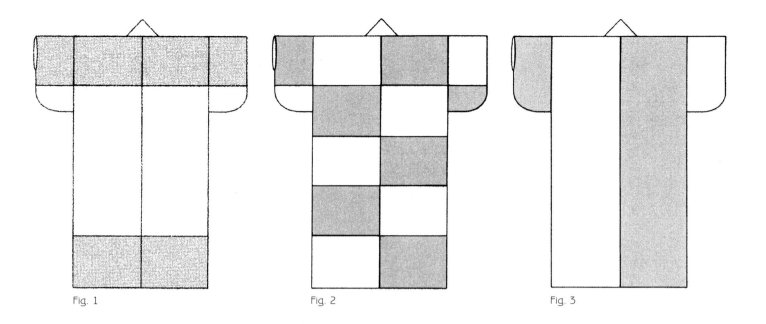

Fig. 1

Fig. 2

Fig. 3

Fig. 1 Defined zones of decoration: *kata suso* (shoulder and hem areas).

Fig. 2 Defined zones of decoration: *dangawari* (alternating horizontal bands or blocks).

Fig. 3 Defined zones of decoration: *katamigawari* (vertical right and left halves of the body).

shapes filling the open spaces. The bright impression of Momoyama-era *kosode* disappeared and was replaced by *kosode* of restrained, quiet tones, whose dynamic designs were elaborate but somewhat somber.

The Keichō *kosode* differed in another aspect. Prior to the Keichō era, *kosode* were mainly made of *nerinuki*, a plain-weave silk composed of warp threads of unglossed silk (gummed; sericin not removed) and weft threads of glossed silk (degummed; sericin removed). These *kosode* had a beautiful sheen and stiffness, like a well-starched shirt.

The major materials of Keichō *kosode*, however, were a plain-weave silk with a twill-weave pattern (*saya*) or monochrome figured satin (*rinzu*). These fabrics and techniques of manufacture had been introduced to Japan from China during the Muromachi period. Their domestic production began in the latter half of the sixteenth century. Both *saya* and *rinzu* were made with glossed silk threads. Unlike *nerinuki* fabric, they are soft and cling to the wearer's body; the silhouette of the soft *kosode* showed every movement. This quality inevitably influenced *kosode* designs. *Nerinuki* silk, with its stiffness, showed very well the zoned compositions, but *saya* and *rinzu* fabrics required new and dynamic designs. The resulting *kosode* of the Kiechō, Genna (1615–1624), and Kanei eras (1624–1644) set a different fashion trend.

Keichō *kosode* were sometimes called *jinashi*, or no-ground designs because small motifs in embroidery and metal foil almost completely filled the ground. The design, fashionable among women in the pleasure quarters in Kyoto, was short-lived. In 1641 (Kanei 18), when the quarter moved from central Kyoto to Shimabara, a western part of Kyoto, the *jinashi* style quickly lost its popularity.

Kanbun-Style Kosode

AROUND THE KANBUN ERA (1661–1673), a new design trend was created. The characteristic abstract background designs of the Keichō *kosode* were transformed into areas with realistic images; the divisions of *somewake* tie-dyeing began to acquire the shapes of mountains or clouds. The zone-division motifs became further diversified to include *noshi* (an auspicious symbol of dried abalone strips tied with ribbon), waves, pines, chrysanthemums, and fans. Eventually these divisions disappeared altogether.

Fig. 4 Typical decorative composition of the Keichō-style *kosode*. Early 17th century. Kanebō Co., Ltd., Osaka.

Fig. 4

After the mid-seventeenth century, this tendency to use realistic images and override design zones became increasingly popular.

Freed from the zone divisions, large motifs were arranged all over the *kosode* in fluid compositions. The *Onhiinagata* (Catalogue) published in 1667 shows that motifs were adopted not only from nature, such as birds and flowers, but also from objects used in everyday life, or scenes from literature, such as famous stories and poems.

On the back of these *kosode* the motifs were arranged as if they were a painting with a unified composition. The motifs were typically arranged on an asymmetrical diagonal axis so that they cascaded from one shoulder to the opposite hem. This popular style of the Kanbun era was called the Kanbun design and, of course, *kosode* with these designs were called Kanbun *kosode*.

Wealthy merchants favored Kanbun *kosode*. Their financial success allowed them to afford these luxurious robes. Through their choices of designs, they expressed their personality, taste, and culture. For example, the Kasasagi design (fig. 5) from the *Onhiinagata*, shows two huge hats (*kasa*) on the upper back and a heron (*sagi*) on a bridge in the lower part. While it can be appreciated merely as a fantastic composition, the design requires the wearer and viewers to possess a good knowledge of classical poetry to correctly interpret the theme.

The words *kasa* (hats) and *sagi* (heron) make up the word *kasasagi* (magpie), a witty pun which further alludes to Tanabata, the popular festival of the weaving goddess and

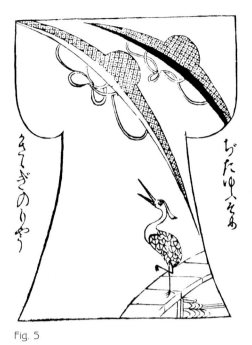

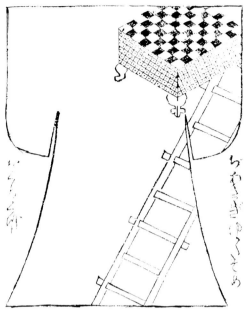

Fig. 5

Fig. 6

her cowherd lover, who live in the sky. The lovers displeased the other gods, and were separated and exiled to remote corners of the heavens. Once a year, on the seventh of July, it is said that the magpies build a bridge across the Milky Way, to help the lovers to meet for a brief time. The Japanese, ancient as well as contemporary, love the story and celebrate the festival, which has inspired poets and artists to produce poems and paintings. Ōtomo no Yakamochi of the eighth century wrote an acclaimed poem, which is included in *Hyakunin Isshu* (Single Poems by 100 Poets):

Kasasagi no	On the bridge like the one in the sky
wataseru hashi ni	built by flying magpies
oku shimo no	the frost is white.
Shiroki o mire ba	I realized
yoru zo fukeni keru	it is late, night has fallen.
Shin Kokin Wakashū	*(New Anthology of Old and New Poems, 1201–1216)*

The *kosode* with a *go* board (*goban*) and a ladder (fig. 6), from the same catalogue, is entitled *Oguri kuzushi*, which alludes to a more contemporary popular story. "Oguri" refers to the famous Oguri Hangan, a fictitious hero in *Jōruri* (a kind of ballad) drama, called "Oguri." It relates the romance of Oguri Hangan and Princess Teru. The parents and brothers of Teru opposed her marriage to Oguri and conspired to kill him; they asked him to ride a wild horse. Since he excelled in the martial arts, not only did he manage to ride the horse, but he also made it do tricks. He made the horse stand on a *go* board with its four feet together and also climb a ladder. The motifs of the game boards and ladder relate to these episodes, and contemporary people would immediately recall the romance.

As we have seen, the repertoire of decorative motifs on Kanbun *kosode* was not limited to flowers and birds or the wind and the moon, but also included literary and allegorical subjects which required viewers with literary knowledge. Furthermore, these motifs were not meant to be seen simply as descriptive ones, but to be enjoyed as witty designs with imaginative interpretations. The bold and high spirit expressed in the Kanbun *kosode* designs echoed the sophisticated spirit of the merchant class, which had succeeded in gaining social recognition through financial success, and whose members had become new arbiters of culture.

The early to mid-Edo period saw a remarkable technical development in dyeing, and it made possible more luxurious *kosode*. Those of the Kanbun era and the subsequent Genroku era (1688–1704) were elaborately decorated with tie-dyeing and further embellished with embroidery in gold and colored threads. *Kanoko* tie-dyed designs, which took enormous amounts of the artisan's time and patience, were much favored for their artistic merits as well as for their sumptuousness.

To control these increasingly luxurious tendencies in clothes, the feudal government frequently attempted to restrict their production. In 1683, the government issued a ban prohibiting the use of gold-figured gauze (*kinsha*) embroidery and *sō-kanoko* in women's *kosode*. *Sō-kanoko* is all-over *kanoko* tie-dyeing, in which the entire surface of the cloth is covered by tiny rows of tie-dyeing. The merchants, however, contrived to make even more beautiful *kosode*, while cleverly avoiding conflict with the law, through the dyeing technique of *yūzen*.

Yūzen Dyeing

Yūzenzome (*yūzen* dyeing) appeared as the result of the merchants' wish to decorate their *kosode* in a spectacular manner. *Yūzen* was the ideal technique because the artist could decorate *kosode* freely, as if they were making paintings, by using fine resist-lines (*itome*) and colors applied with a brush.

Yūzenzome flourished around the Genroku period, when the merchant culture reached its highest level. The key figure in creating this trend was Miyazaki Yūzen (?–1758), a famous fan painter residing in front of the Chion-in Temple in the Higashiyama district of Kyoto. Yūzen's fan paintings were highly favored; they were mentioned in stories written by Ihara Saikaku (1642–1693) and were greatly in demand. Yūzen designed *kosode* in the style of his paintings, which dyers then produced using the technique that came to be called *yūzenzome*.

A *kosode* catalogue published in 1687, *Genji hiinakata* (Genji Catalogue) mentions that *yūzenzome* was used not only in fans but also on *kosode*, verifying that the *yūzenzome* design was popular on both *kosode* and fans. In 1688 another catalogue, *Yūzen hiinakata*, was published. In the preface the author wrote that this *yūzen* style was in fashion both among noble ladies who had never been exposed to the sun as well as among young country girls who worked in the mud. Such exaggerated advertisements in these fashion books only served to stimulate demand for this new style and technique. Through the catalogues, *yūzenzome* instantly became the most sought-after style of the Genroku period.

The *yūzen* dyeing process as it was practiced during the Genroku period is not clearly understood. After that period, the technique and process were improved from time to time, and became more complex. The practice of *yūzenzome* today is as follows. Unlike rice-paste resist-decorated textiles (*tsutsugaki*), seen in the Muromachi period

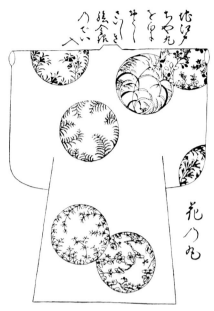

Fig. 7

Fig. 7 *Flowers in Medallions* from the *Yūzen hiinakata*, 1688.

and later, *yūzenzome*-decorated textiles are not immersed in dye vats. Rather, very fine outlines of the design are drawn using a brush and tracing fluid on a smooth, starched length of silk. These lines are then covered with rice-paste resist using a tube with a fine hollow point (*tsutsu*). The entire cloth is covered with a mordant to prevent the lines from blurring. Next, the details of the design are painted in, using a brush and various colored dyes. These colored designs are then covered with rice paste. Finally, the cloth is brushed with dye to color the background, steamed to fix the dyes, and thoroughly washed to remove the tracing fluid and the rice paste.

Around the Genroku period, the ground dyeing might have been done first, unlike the modern process. Neither is it clear whether steaming was employed to fix the dyes. The present *yūzenzome* technique is extremely complex, making the finished fabrics very expensive. *Yūzen* dyeing in the early phase, however, might have been simpler, and so perhaps was not then considered expensive.

The fine, threadlike line achieved by paste-resist, a characteristic of *yūzenzome*, had earlier been used in the Muromachi and Momoyama periods. The preface to *Yūzen hiinakata* (Yūzen Catalogue), however, mentions technical improvements in the dyeing technique: "The dyes do not bleed in water and they look soft on any silk"; and, "It had been impossible to dye *momi* [vermilion-colored plain-weave silk] because it bleeds, but now we can paint it with painting pigments." *Yūzenzome* gained an expansive popularity using this improved technique, which was also used on fashionable *yūzen* fan paintings. Thus the *yūzen kosode* style was harmoniously unified in both traditional and new fashions. As *Yūzen hiinagata* commented, while the style had "classical refinements," it also had a "delicate current style which appeals to people who like new things."

One popular *yūzen* design was flowers in medallions (fig. 7). But by 1692, as *Onna chōhōki* (Convenient References for Women) mentions, the styles of Kyoto *kosode* changed, and "*Yūzen* medallions with flowers fell out of fashion." In an effort to meet

Fig. 8

Fig. 9

Fig. 8 *Kosode* with of horse-race scene at the Kamigamo Shrine. From the *Tōryū moyō hiinagata tsuru no koe*, 1724.

Fig. 9
Shiroagari design from the *Hiinagata tsugiho sakura*, 1758.

the demands of the time, *yūzenzome* was compelled to change. *Yosei hiinakata* (Yosei Catalogue), written by Yūzen himself in 1692, showed designs very much like paintings, such as "carp climbing over waterfalls" or mountain landscapes. *Yūzenzome's* main strength was this ability to execute designs that looked like painting on fabrics, which had not been possible using traditional dyeing techniques. Its popularity continues into the twentieth century.

The *kosode* with a horse-race scene at the Kamigamo Shrine (cat. no. 13) shows a painting-like design in a dynamic composition. A very similar design is included in the *kosode* catalogue *Tōryū moyō hiinagata tsuru no koe* (Catalogue of Current Designs: Cry of a Crane) published in 1724 (fig. 8).

The catalogue *Wakoku hiinagata taizen* (A Collection of Japanese Catalogues), published in 1698, gives a glimpse of the *yūzenzome* trend in *kosode* catalogues: 19 out of 116 designs, or less than 20 percent, were described with captions such as *yūzenzome*, *yūzen irosashi* (filling an outlined patterns with colors in *yūzen*), and *yūzen irobokashi* (gradual shading of color in *yūzen*). But in *Shōtoku hiinagata* (Catalogue of the Shōtoku Period), published in 1713, 46 *yūzenzome* out of 96 designs were shown, and in the following year, in *Hiinagata Gion bayashi* (Catalogue of the Gion Quarter) there were 65 *yūzen* designs out of 144 illustrations. This documents an increasingly higher percentage of *yūzenzome* over about 15 years. It appears that *yūzenzome* reached its peak of popularity during 1714; subsequently, from the middle to latter half of the eighteenth century, *yūzenzome* designs occupied only about 20 percent of such catalogues. Although *yūzenzome* designs had not overwhelmed the fashion current, they still remained solidly popular. But after the second half of the eighteenth century, catalogues began to show new trends; designs described as *shiroagari* (white-reserved designs) and *shiroage nuiiri* (white-reserved designs and embroidery) began to outnumber *yūzenzome* ones.

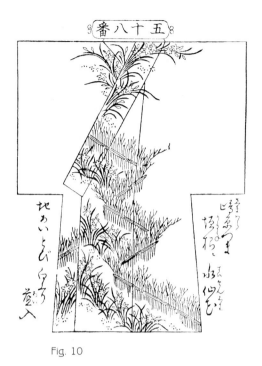

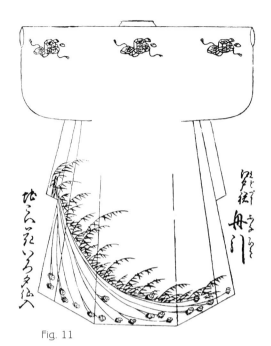

Fig. 10

Fig. 11

Shiroagari Design

As DECORATIVE COMPOSITIONS on *kosode* changed (as will be explained later), new decorative techniques were pursued. One of them was the white-reserved design (*shiroage* or *shiroagari,* white-reserved design on a monochrome ground). Unlike the bold designs with large motifs of the previous periods, smaller motifs were executed in white reserve using paste resist against a monochrome ground (fig. 9). In order to make them stand out, the ground colors were inevitably dark, like deep blue, indigo blue, or dark green. Sometimes additional embroidery (*shiroage nuiiri*) was used, not for a showy effect, but to add a modest element of color. The robes decorated in *shiroage* presented a world of monochrome distinctly different from the multicolored designs of the previous periods.

A taste for simplicity, as seen in the *shiroage* designs, began to manifest itself around 1751–1763, suggesting that the mid-eighteenth century was the turning point. The change cannot be attributed to a simple chronological development, but to historical circumstances. At this time the center of art and culture shifted from the Kyoto-Osaka region to the relatively new city, Edo (present-day Tokyo), where the seat of the shogunal government was located. In Edo, subdued taste (*iki*) in design was more valued, and was to become the predominant taste during the late Edo period. *Kosode* with *shiroage* designs marked a new period of simplicity in costume design.

Shift in Design Focus from the Back to the Front of Women's Appearance

DECORATIVE COMPOSITIONS on *kosode* were closely related to accessories and hairstyles. These interacted to create fashion trends. A sash (*obi*) was an essential accessory for dressing in *kosode.* At first only a narrow cord, *obi* became increasingly wider, and by the Genroku era (1688–1703) had typically become 20 cm (ca. 7¾ in.) wide. This resulted in dividing the *kosode* designs into upper and lower halves. The Kanbun compositions, with their all-over patterns of large motifs, began to be split in this way (called split designs), or else the decoration was limited only to the lower half (called half designs). This tendency further shifted the design focus from the back of the *kosode* to the front.

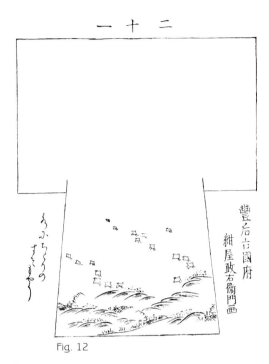

Fig. 12

Fig. 13

Opposite

Fig. 10 *Shimabara tsuma* from the *Shin hiinagata akebono sakura*, 1781.

Fig. 11 *Edozuma* design from the *Hiinagata sode no Yama*, 1757.

Above

Fig. 12 *Suso moyō* from the *Shin hiinagata chitose sode*, 1800.

Fig. 13 *Ura moyō* from the *Hiinagata chitose no sode Yama*, 1757.

This tendency created localized compositions in front areas: designs over the neckband to the skirt (*Shimabara tsuma*; fig. 10); designs from lower edge of the neckband to the skirt (*Edozuma*; fig. 11), and hem designs (*suso moyō*; fig. 12), or even designs on the lining, where the lining of the front hem was decorated (*ura moyō*; fig. 13). During the Horeki era (1751–1763), early examples of *Edozuma* designs emerged, and many examples appeared in the Meiwa to Tenmei eras (1764–1788). *Shimabara tsuma* were exemplified in *Shin hiinagata akebono sakura* (New Catalogue: Cherry Blossoms in Dawn; 1781). Many examples of *suso moyō* designs appeared during the Meiwa (1764–1772) era and the Bunka (1804–1818) and Bunsei (1818–1830) eras.

Just as much as the wider sashes influenced the creation of new compositions, changing hair styles also influenced *kosode* designs. *Han moyō*, or half-designs, were localized on the lower half of the *kosode* from the waist down and appeared after the Genroku era, a trend related to enlarged hair styles such as the Shimada style (cat. no. 63). The tied hair styles of the Edo period began with the back hair chignon (*tsuto*), a forelock of hair tied at the top (*maegami*), and developed to expand locks at the side of the head (*bin*).

During the early to the mid-Edo period, the hair did not protrude from the sides of the face but was pulled toward the back chignon, which hung prominently low on the neck. When the volume of the hair style was concentrated on the back of the head, the *kosode* compositions were also focused on the back of the garment, as in Kanbun and Genroku period *kosode*. The entire art of dressing emphasized the back: the hair, the *kosode* design, and the tied sash all focused on the back. Paintings of beautiful women emphasized their backs, as seen in many paintings depicting them in postures of turning to look back, paintings now known as "beauties looking back."

During the later period, the sidelocks of hair expanded outward from the head, and the back chignons were reduced in size, making the front view more important.

Fig. 14 A woman
of the samurai class
in *koshimaki*-style
dressing

The use of elaborate combs and hairpins called even more attention to the frontal view. At the same time, the sash became as wide as 30 cm (11¾ in.), and the *kosode* design's focal point was lowered to the hem line. Thus the woman looked well balanced at her head, waist, and feet.

Samurai
Class
Dress for
Women

THE FASHION TRENDS of the Edo period, led by the merchant class, caused the invention of new designs and techniques of dyeing. Designs blossomed with striking decorative compositions of large motifs. In comparison, the samurai class and imperial court circles were conservative, clinging to tradition. Over time, however, they were influenced by contemporary fashions and began to adopt some aspects of current trends. Through their choice of design motifs and manner of dressing, they established their own fashion trends.

In 1615, immediately after the establishment of the Tokugawa Bakufu, the shogunate office issued *Buke sho-hatto* (Laws for the Military Houses), laws promulgated for samurai and daimyo. Thirteen articles prescribed the conduct of the military class, including aspects of their personal lives such as marriage and dress. Following the law, dress codes for women in the shogun's inner castle (*ōoku*) were also established. The two kinds of robes characteristically worn by women of the samurai class were *uchikake*, used in winter, and *koshimaki*, used in summer. The use of these robes began in the Muromachi period, but the manner of dressing became more stylized in the Edo period.

Uchikake are also *kosode*, but worn as outer garments over *kosode*, like cloaks, without a sash. They were worn from September 9th to the last day of March in the lunar calendar. *Kosode* worn under *uchikake* were called middle robes (*aigi*) and were made with figured satin (*rinzu*); *obi* tied over the *aigi* were called *kakeshita obi* (*obi* under *uchikake*; cat. nos. 41, 42), and they measured ca. 20–28 cm (7 ¾ to 11 in.). They were made of heavy materials such as velvet or satin, and were decorated with embroidery.

Koshimaki, for formal summer dressing, were worn from April 1 to September 8 in the lunar calendar. *Koshimaki*-style dressing originated in the Muromachi period when *uchikake* were slipped off the shoulders and tied around the waist. In the Edo period, this *koshimaki* style changed; instead of being wrapped around the waist, the garments were tied with a sash 11 cm. wide, with each end 30 to 60 cm long. These ends were made stiff with interfacing, so that when they were tied, they formed two wings on either side, through which the *koshimaki* sleeves were placed (fig. 14).

The material used for *koshimaki* were lightweight, unglossed *nerinuki* silks appropriate to summer wear. The fabrics were dyed a reddish black and were finely embroidered in an all-over pattern of auspicious symbols, such as the myriad treasures, plum sprays, cranes, and turtles.

In mid summer, after May 5, silk *kosode* (*aigi*) were replaced by *katabira* made of ramie. The characteristic motifs used to decorate summer ramie *katabira* were taken from classical poems, stories, and well-known sites referred to in famous poems, all of which had associations with imperial culture. At the time there was no term for this group of motifs, but later they began to be called *goshodoki* (lit. clearing up the imperial themes). It might sound odd that women of the samurai class favored imperial motifs, but they intended to display their high cultural and educational background in the classics. These women tried to acquire culture and elegance comparable to the ladies in the imperial circles. The *goshodoki* motifs included flowers of the four seasons, palaces and pavilions, streams, imperial carriages, brushwood fences, as well as other objects and scenes that suggested classical literature and Noh drama. All of these nostalgic motifs suggested the golden age of Japanese classics, as represented by *The Tale of Genji*.

Among the women working in the shogunal apartment (*ōoku*) of the Edo castle, those ranked above ladies-in-waiting had some choice in the designs of their garments: figured satin (*rinzu*) in white, black, or red with embroidered decorations of flowers in four seasons arranged in bouquets, or sprays of flowers combined with woven patterns of rising serpentine (*tatewaku*), interlocking circles (*shippō tsunagi*), and swastika.

Robes of Imperial Court Nobles

THE CLOTHING STYLE of imperial court nobles was firmly established in the Heian period. After that time, the tradition continued with some modifications. For the most formal ceremonies, such as for coronations, emperors wore ceremonial robes that had been prescribed in the dress code (*Ifukuryō* established during the years 718 to 722). For regular annual events, they wore full court robes, but for everyday life, they wore *noshi, kariginu* (lit. hunting cloth), or *ko-nōshi* (cat. no. 24), an informal *nōshi* in the *kariginu* style with a horizontal decorative band around the hem.

Characteristic features of court robes for both men and women are the wide sleeves with wide wrist openings which extend the entire sleeve length (cat. nos. 23, 24). The main difference between women's and men's robes was that the men's robes were double-breasted and had a round neck opening.

The decorations on imperial fabrics were usually woven and seldom achieved by dyeing. Imperial women wore *jūnihitoe* (the many-layered court robe) for the most formal ceremonies, but their garments had far more variety than the men's robes. From the mid-Edo period, *kosode* and *uchikake* (called *kaitori* in imperial circles) began to be used. They were called "current styles."

The adoption of *kosode* into the imperial court has been attributed to the marriage of Masako (later called Tōfukumon-in: 1607–1678), the daughter of Tokugawa Hidetada, the second shogun, to the emperor Go-Mizunoo. She brought costumes of the samurai class into the imperial household. The ledgers of Kariganeya, a dry-goods store in Kyoto, record many custom orders of *kosode* and *katabira* by Tōfukumon-in. Kariganeya's ledgers also indicate that these *kosode* were in the Kanbun style, popular among commoners. Court ladies gradually established their own styles executed in techniques of their own choice. During the late Edo period, *kosode* were decorated with elegant traditional motifs of flowers and birds, such as cranes, which alluded to ancient poems. These motifs were often executed in embroidery.

The Prince Takamatsu Collection of Imperial Robes in the Kyoto National Museum

THE PRINCE TAKAMATSU COLLECTION was a gift from Princess Takamatsu, wife of the late Prince Takamatsu (1905–1987), the younger brother of the Emperor Shōwa (1901–1989), to the Agency for Cultural Property of Japan. It is now housed in the Kyoto National Museum. The collection was originally owned by the Arisugawa family, a princely household established by Prince Yorihito (1603–1638), the seventh son of Emperor Go-Yōsei (1571–1617). At the time Yorihito established an independent household, he was residing at the Takamatsu Palace; hence his title, Prince Takamatsu.

Prince Nagahito (1637–1685), sixth son of Emperor Go-Mizunoo (1596–1680) succeeded the lineage. When he became the Emperor Gōsai, his second son Yukihito (1656–1699) became head of the family. The household title, Takamatsu, changed to Prince Arisugawa. It continued through ten generations, to the Meiji period. The Arisugawa family ceased to exist because the tenth family head did not have an heir. But in 1923, by Emperor Taisho's order, his third son Nobuhito was named Prince Takamatsu, and he continued to head the family and conduct ceremonies for the house of Arisugawa. Because of these historical circumstances, the Arisugawa collection came to include robes of the emperors Go-Mizunoo, Reigen, Kōkaku, Ninkō, and Kōmei, and princely robes of the fifth head, Prince Yorihito (1713–1769); the sixth head, Prince Orihito (1753–1820); the eighth head, Prince Takahito (1812–1886); and the ninth head, Prince Naruhito (1835–95), for a total of ninety-eight items. All of these robes are made of beautifully woven fabrics. The date and the owner of each robe is known, and thus they form an invaluable source of information for the study of costumes in general, and of court nobles' clothes in particular.

The ninety-eight robes are divided into two groups—adult and children's robes. The adult male robes includes ceremonial robes such as *hō* (a formal ceremonial garment), *nōshi, ko-nōshi, sashinuki* trousers, and football jackets (*mari suikan*). The Arisugawa collection does not includes *kariginu*, which were used by emperors for informal robes. But it does contain fifteen *ko-nōshi*, including those of the two retired emperors, Kokau and Ninko, and also of Prince Takahito, made in July 1882. *Ko-nōshi* were informal robes used for outings by retired emperors, princes, and or other high ranking officials, such as ministers and generals of the Imperial Guard. It is likely that *ko-nōshi* were used as private robes instead of *kariginu*.

The group of children's clothing includes *warawa nōshi* (cat. no. 27), *hanjiri* (an upper garment with a short back panel; cat. no. 29), *omeshi* (princely *furisode*) and a girl's *hosonaga* (cat. no. 30). These were used by children in ceremonies such as Fukasogi and Chakko.

The Tamura Shizuko Collection in the Kyoto National Museum

ASSEMBLED BY MRS. SHIZUKO TAMURA, a businesswoman of Kyoto, this collection includes a wide range of items related to dressing: *kosode*, accessories, and toiletry articles loved and used by people of all classes, including daughters of the daimyo and the children of commoners. Some are extremely extravagant, such as *maki-e* lacquer wares or plain garments of ikat.

Mrs. Tamura established the Tamura Shiryōkan Museum in 1989, in a southern part of Kyoto, to house her extensive collections and to display them under various themes. In 1994, to commemorate Kyoto's 1200th anniversary and her museum's fifth anniversary, a portion of her collections was donated to the Kyoto National Museum. The donation includes 60 cosmetic utensils, 230 hair ornaments, 170 *kosode* and children's robes, and 200 advertisement flyers of the Meiji period (1867–1911). The most distinguished group is the children's robes. Adorable baby clothes and *furisode* of commoners' children together with the robes of court nobles and samurai families provide excellent materials to appreciate and study the clothing customs and dyeing techniques of the Edo and post-Edo periods.

The collection of cosmetic utensils includes items used by daughters of daimyo and a few lacquerwares in the style of Kōdaiji *maki-e*, *maki-e* boxes, *fusego*, and incense burners of the Edo period.

The collection of hair ornaments also includes the finest quality of combs in *maki-e* lacquer and tortoiseshell as well as an extensive selection of hairpins and dangling ornaments with interesting designs, all of the finest craftsmanship. Superbly crafted beautiful pins in gold, silver, and coral were fashionable among young girls during the Bunka (1804–1818) and Bunsei (1818–1830) eras of the Edo period, when the culture had fully matured.

CHANGING FASHIONS

1

Dōfuku (samurai coat) with
Paulownias and Arrows
Tsujigahana dyeing on white *nerinuki*
  ground
Silk
Momoyama period, 16th century
IMPORTANT CULTURAL PROPERTY

This coat is famous for its provenance.
Once owned by Toyotomi Hideyoshi
(1537–1598), one of the three warlords
who competed to consolidate war-torn
Japan, it was given to a vassal of Nanbu
Nobunao (1546–1599). The vassal Kita
Saemon-no-Jō Nobuchika took horses
and falcons to Hideyoshi during the
Odawara campaign against the Hōjō
family in 1590. The campaign was
important for Hideyoshi because its
victory enabled him to complete the
military reunification of Japan and to
establish a new feudal hierarchy with
Hideyoshi himself at its head.

    On the ground of white, lustrous,
plain-weave silk (*nerinuki*), the decorative motifs are executed in the stitched
tie-dyeing technique (*shibori*) called
tsujigahana. The purple shoulder band is
patterned with paulownia blossoms, the
origin of Hideyoshi's family crest (*mon*),
in white reserve, created by means of
shibori; the green lower border and its
feathered arrow shafts were reserved in
white by the same technique. The broad
white area between the bands is scattered
with paulownia blossoms in light blue
and green. The arrows in a rigid row and
the loosely scattered paulownia blossoms
make a bold design, contrasting static
and dynamic forces.

    Nerinuki is a plain-weave fabric with
raw silk warps and degummed silk wefts,
and was the favorite material for
tsujigahana. Degumming silk thread
means to remove sericin, the sticky
substance that adheres to the silk
filaments unwound from cocoons.

                     SK

1–1. *Dōfuku*. *Nerinuki,* a plain-weave fabric with raw silk
warps and degummed silk wefts. The densely woven
fabric has a characteristic luster and stiffness. (Detail)

1-2. *Dōfuku*. The trace of the stitching of stitch-resist tie
dyeing *(nuishime)* used in *tsujigahana* dyeing technique.
(Detail)

1-3. *Dōfuku*. Hemp thread used in stitch-resist tie dyeing
is left unpulled so the thick thread does not damage the
fabric. (Detail)

Pl. 1

2
Kosode with Flowering Plants
Embroidery and gold leaf on white
 nerinuki ground
Silk
Momoyama period, 16th century
IMPORTANT CULTURAL PROPERTY

The entire *kosode* is divided in alternating bands of floral patterns. The plum
blossoms of spring, wisteria of summer,
maples of autumn, and snow-laden
bamboo leaves of winter are executed in
a combination of embroidery and
metallic leaf application (*nuihaku*, lit.
embroidery and metal leaf). These
motifs are rendered in long-stitched
embroidery, and the spaces between
them are filled with gold leaf (*surihaku*)
applied by adhesive.

   Although these lively plants and
flowers are not always naturalistically
depicted, they capture the characteristics of each.

   The long embroidery stitches in
nuihaku are called *watashi-nui*
(crossing). They can span the breadth
of individual motifs, and well match
the powerful design that flourished
during the period from the end of the
Muromachi to the Momoyama period
(1573–1615).

                    SK

Pl. 2

PI. 3

3

Okuni Kabuki
Six-fold screen; ink, colors, and
  gold on paper
Momoyama period, 17th century
IMPORTANT CULTURAL PROPERTY

In 1603 a woman called Okuni and
her troupe started to perform dances
and comical plays in the precincts of
the Kitano Tenjin Shrine in Kyoto,
inaugurating the kabuki theatrical
form. Kabuki is one of the three
major classical theatrical forms in
modern Japan, together with Noh and
bunraku (puppet theater). The young
and beautiful Okuni, a native of
Izumo province (present-day
Shimane prefecture), performed in a

costume of an extraordinary style,
which was considered "outrageous" or
"outlaw" by the contemporary public
at that time.

This screen painting illustrates
Okuni's theater in great detail. On a
stage which imitates that of a Noh
theater, Okuni is dancing in a black
short coat with her sword on her
shoulder, accompanied by musicians
with drums and flutes at the back of
the stage. Many spectators, men and

women, old and young, surround
the stage. This screen, an extremely
important work, represents the early
phase of Kabuki theatrical art as
well as the costume fashions of the
seventeenth century.

HK

4

Kosode with "Pine Bark" Lozenges
and Flowers
Tie-dyeing, embroidery, and gold leaf
  on figured satin (*rinzu*) ground
Silk
Edo period, 17th century
IMPORTANT CULTURAL PROPERTY

During the first half of the seventeenth
century, which included the Keichō
(1596–1614), Genna (1615–1624), and
Kanei (1624–1644) eras, popular kosode
designs were created by means of
somewake (a background divided into
different color zones) tie-dyeing, and
were filled with fine motifs, such as
small flowers in embroidery and gold
leaf application. Such *kosode* were called
Keichō -style *kosode.*

   In Keichō -style *kosode*, the ground
was established by *somewake* tie-dyeing
in solid black, red, or white. Then the
kosode were decorated with small
embroidered motifs and further filled
with clouds of gold leaf. In addition to
the flowers, trees, and birds, the
geometric motifs of lozenge diapers
enclosing smaller lozenges (*irikobishi*)
filled the ground extensively, making a
crowded and complex general impression. Due to this treatment of the
background colors and details, the
Keichō -style *kosode* looks dark and
heavy despite the extensive use of gold
leaf. This impression contrasts with the
brighter appearance presented by earlier
kosode of the Momoyama period of the
sixteenth century, which are similarly
decorated with gold leaf.

   In addition, this complex tie-dyeing
technique and the treatment of the
design motifs points to a new stylistic
trend that was occurring in the early
seventeenth century.

                                    SK

Pl. 5

5

Dancers

Six-fold screen; ink, colors, and gold
  on paper

Edo period, 17th century

Property of Kyoto City

IMPORTANT CULTURAL PROPERTY

Each holding a fan, six female dancers
perform against a plain gold background. Unlike the *Okuni Kabuki*
screen (cat. no. 3), this painting focuses
on the individual dancers, who were
courtesans, with detailed observations
of their costumes and coiffures.
Although there is no suggestion of an
interior setting, the gold background
hints that a splendid party is going on
in the gay quarters, and we may
imagine that the viewers are positioned
as if they were seated in a room before
the dancers, appreciating their exquisite
performances. The costume designs,
the narrow *obis*, and the unbound hair
styles date the painting to around the
seventeenth century.

HK

6

A Beauty Standing on a Balcony

Hanging scroll; ink and color on paper

Edo period, 17th century

Beautifully dressed, a woman stands
on a balcony and gazes dreamily into
the distance. The identity of this beauty
is hinted at by her *kosode* design of
bridges, grouped in several variations
(Yatsuhashi, "Eight Bridges"). This
motif recalls an episode from the *Tales
of Ise* of the early Heian period (794–
1185), the main part of which includes
the poetic biography of the hero
Ariwara no Narihira (825–880), an
acclaimed poet. Narihira, on a journey
to the eastern provinces, arrived at a
village called Yatsuhashi in Mikawa
province (present-day Chiryū City of
Aichi prefecture). There he longingly
recalled the woman he had left in
Kyoto. Her loose hair, the *kosode*
with large decorative motifs, and
the narrow *obi* suggest a date in the
seventeenth century.

HK

Pl. 6

7

Katabira (summer *kosode*) with
Chrysanthemums and Hemp Leaves
Kanoko shibori dyeing and embroidery
  on dark-brown ground
Ramie (*asa*)
Edo period, 17th century

Kosode made of ramie (*asa*) were called
katabira and were used for summer
wear. The bold design of hemp leaves
on this *katabira* of fine ramie is
concentrated on the right-hand side, a
characteristic of the so-called Kanbun
period (1661–1673) style. A page from
a *kosode* catalogue, *Onhiinagata*,
published in 1667, shows a design
similar to this example. A note in the
catalogue explains that the widely
spread petals are, in fact, leaves of
hemp-palms, and the fan-shaped
motifs below them are chrysanthemums seen in a side view.

  The techniques of the dyeing and
embroidery further reveal characteristics of the Kanbun-style *kosode*. The
kanoko shibori ("fawn-spots" dyeing)
are even and small and are of a variety
called *honhitta* (lit. real *hitta*), which
have small, squared spots with dots in
the ground color in the center of each
spot. The embroidery was executed
softly with untwisted threads.

  Katabira (lit. one side) is a
lightweight, unlined summer *kosode*.
Before the Edo period, unlined *kosode*
included those of silk and cotton,
but later the term *katabira* came to be
used exclusively for summer robes of
ramié (bleached *kibira*) made in Nara
(*Narazarashi*) and ramie (*karamushi*)
made in Echigo (*Echigo jōfu*).

Hemp and ramie were suitable fibers for
summer robes because of their ability to
absorb moisture and dry quickly, and
because of their pleasant texture on the
skin in humid weather.

  Kanoko shibori is a tie-dye technique
in which clusters of spots to be reserved
are tightly wrapped before dyeing. Each
spot has a smaller dot of the background
color in the center. The result recalls the
spots on a fawn, hence the name.
Sometimes the term *kanoko shibori* is
used interchangeably with the term *hitta*;
but *hitta* may be used specifically to refer
to clusters of square spots.

  SK

7. *Katabira. Kanoko shibori* ("fawn-spots") dyeing), tiny tie
dyeing on plain-weave ground. (Detail)

Pl. 7

8

Kosode with Flowing Streams and
Chrysanthemums
Tie-dyeing and embroidery on white,
  figured-satin (*rinzu*) ground
Silk
Edo period, 18th century

The design consists of flowing streams
and chrysanthemums arranged in zigzag
patterns over which Chinese characters
are scattered randomly on the shoulders
and sleeves. These motifs are rendered by
tie-dyeing and embroidery.

   The design recalls the poem *Kiku*
(Chrysanthemum) by Sugawara no
Fumitoki (899–981), recorded in *Wakan
rōeishū* (Anthology of Japanese and
Chinese Poems) complied in 1012:

Rankeien no	The imperial garden
arashi no	with orchids
Murasaki o kudaku	After the storm
nochi	blew away
	their purple flowers
Hōraitō no tsuki no	Only chrysanthe-
	mums remained,
shimo o terasu uchi	illuminated by the
	moon in the frost

The strong design, with motifs cascading
from the right shoulder to the left skirt
and leaving the left waist area empty,
reflects the characteristic style of the
Genroku period (1688–1704).

                              SK

9

Kosode with Reeds and *Jakago*
(gabions)
Resist dyeing and embroidery on
  light-yellow crepe (*chirimen*) ground
Silk
Edo period, 18th century

The design units on this *kosode*
combine windblown reeds with the
jakago or gabion, large bamboo baskets
filled with gravel used to reinforce
riverbanks. The motifs are executed by
means of stencil-resist dye together
with additional embroidery.

　By scattering the motifs on the
back of the kosode from the right
shoulder to the lower left, the design
creates a reversed "C" pattern, leaving
the left waist area empty. This composition goes back to the Kanbun era
(1661–1671) of the Edo period.
Although the general color scheme is
subdued, the dynamic forms of the
decorative motifs and the embroidery
in gold thread on the light ground
make this garment strikingly bold.

SK

10 (following page)

Kosode with Landscape of Plum
Trees in Snow
Paste-resist dyeing and embroidery on
  blue crepe (*chirimen*) ground
Silk
Edo period, 18th century

This design was inspired by a *waka* poem
by Chūnagon (Court Secretary) Asatada
(910–966). It was included in the
anthology *Shūi wakashū*, compiled
during the years between 1005 to 1007:

Uguisu no	Without the singing
koe nakariseba	of a nightingale
Yuki kienu	in a snow-covered
yamazato ikade	village,
Haru o shiramashi	How would one know
	spring has come?

On the upper back, the characters of
the poem are embroidered in gold
thread and are scattered over a snow-
covered village. On the lower back, plum
trees, a symbol of spring and joy, allude
to a nightingale.

　Along with embroidery, the
decorative motifs were created in white
reserve on the blue ground. Called
shiroage nuiiri (white reserve supplemented with embroidery), it is a style of
yūzen dyeing in which the pattern is
reserved in white by means of paste-resist,
then supplemented with touches of bright
embroidery. *Shiroage kosode* were
frequently featured in *kosode* design
catalogues of the mid-eighteenth century.
This white-reserve dye technique appears
to have come into vogue at this time,
replacing the more complicated *yūzen*
technique that had been preferred since
the seventeenth century.

SK

11 (following page)

Kosode with Fences (*shibagaki*) and
Small Chrysanthemums
Paste-resist dyeing and embroidery on
  light-blue crepe (*chirimen*) ground
Silk
Edo period, 18th century

On the light-blue ground the
chrysanthemums and fences are
reserved in white by means of paste-
resist, then supplemented with
embroidery. The motifs are spread
along the lower edges of the neck-
bands (*tsuma*) to the skirt. This kind
of design is known as *Edozuma*
(design around the *tsuma* popular in
the city of Edo), and began to be
popular in Edo around the Meiwa era
(1764–1772).

　Tsuma moyō azuma hiinagata
(Catalogue of Edo-Style Designs of
Tsuma), published in 1769, included
many *kosode* of *Edozuma* styles.
Subdued *Edozuma* designs were used
primarily for *tomesode*, *kosode* with
regular sleeve length (ca. 55 cm) for
married women.

　The border design of this *kosode*
is likewise quiet, decorated with
repeated small motifs scattered all
over. The technique of white reserve
achieved by paste-resist suggests the
date of this *kosode* at around the
second half of the eighteenth century.

SK

Pl. 9

12

Uchikake (outer *kosode*) with Rough
Seacoast and Tortoises
Embroidery on blue *nanako*-weave
 ground
Silk
Edo period, 19th century

An *uchikake* is an outer *kosode* worn
unbelted as a cloak. The design composition exhibits the bilateral symmetry
typical of the late Edo style. The garment
is decorated in the border around the
hem with turtles swimming in rolling
waves. The same design appears on the
lining of the skirt. This *uchikake*
exemplifies the popular trend during the
early nineteenth century of decorating
the lining with motifs matching the
design on the garment's exterior.
    The silk ground of this *uchikake* is
woven in a variation of plain weave
(*hira-ori*) called *nanako* (lit. fish eggs),
where a set of two warp threads cross the
thicker weft thread, making a texture
that resembles fish eggs lying in a row.
There exist several other examples of
formal nineteenth-century *kosode* made
with the same type of woven silk and
decorated with auspicious symbols.
                                          SK

12. *Uchikake.* A type of plain weave called *nanako* (lit.
fish eggs). A set of two warps crosses the thicker weft
threads. The texture resembles fish eggs lying in a row.
(Detail)

Pl. 12

YŪZENZOME

13

Kosode for a Male Child with
Horse-racing at Kamigamo Shrine
Yūzen dyeing and embroidery on
  white crepe (*chirimen*) ground
Silk
Edo period, 18th century

The Shinto ceremony of racing horses
at the Kamigamo Shrine in the
northern part of Kyoto is held annually
on the fifth of May. Two horses
compete in the race. They dash from
the starting line, marked by a cherry
tree, and finish at a maple tree at the
far end of the grounds.

   This ceremonial race began
centuries ago during the Heian period
(794–1185), as a prayer for good
harvests. For the competition, the
fastest horses were selected from the
provincial estates (*shōen*) of temples,
shrines, and the aristocracy.

   The upper portion of the back of
this boy's *kosode* is decorated with a
diagonally placed checkered pattern of
red and white, below which the horse-
race scene takes place against a
background of maple trees. The two
competing horses are shown dashing
toward the goal. *Yūzen* dyeing power-
fully renders this scene in fine detail;
each form is outlined with fine white
lines (*itome*) achieved by means of
paste-resist.

                                        SK

13-1. *Kosode.* A crepe *(chirimen)* made by S-and Z-twisted
threads. *Chirimen* is a heavily textured silk crepe produced by
plain weave with untwisted warps and strongly twisted wefts
whose twist direction alternates. The tension between the
warps and wefts in different directions causes a crinkled
surface. (Detail)

13-2. *Kosode. Yūzen* dyeing on white silk crepe showing the
thin resist lines *(itome).* (Detail)

Pl. 13

14

Kosode with Dutch Rushes, Flowers, and Rabbits
Yūzen dyeing and embroidery on white
 and red crepe (*chirimen*) ground
Silk
Edo period, 18th century

This *kosode*'s ground alternates in two-colored horizontal bands created by the *shibori* technique (*somewake*), with decoration added by means of *yūzen* dyeing and embroidery. In the white bands, Dutch rushes are depicted intermingled with decorative ovals, which enclose the traditional combination of rabbits and flowers or waves.

In textiles imported from Ming China, this combination of rabbits and flowers, usually enclosed in circles, is commonly seen. The *kosode* design book *Tōfū bijo hiinagata* (Catalogue of Current Beauties), published in 1727, included some examples of rabbits in medallions, attesting that this motif was then becoming popular. On the other hand, the combination of rabbits and waves could also derive from a Japanese Noh play, *Chikubushima*. But despite the obvious connection with Chinese or Japanese classical sources, this design of rabbits placed in white and red bands on this *kosode* looks amazingly modern.

SK

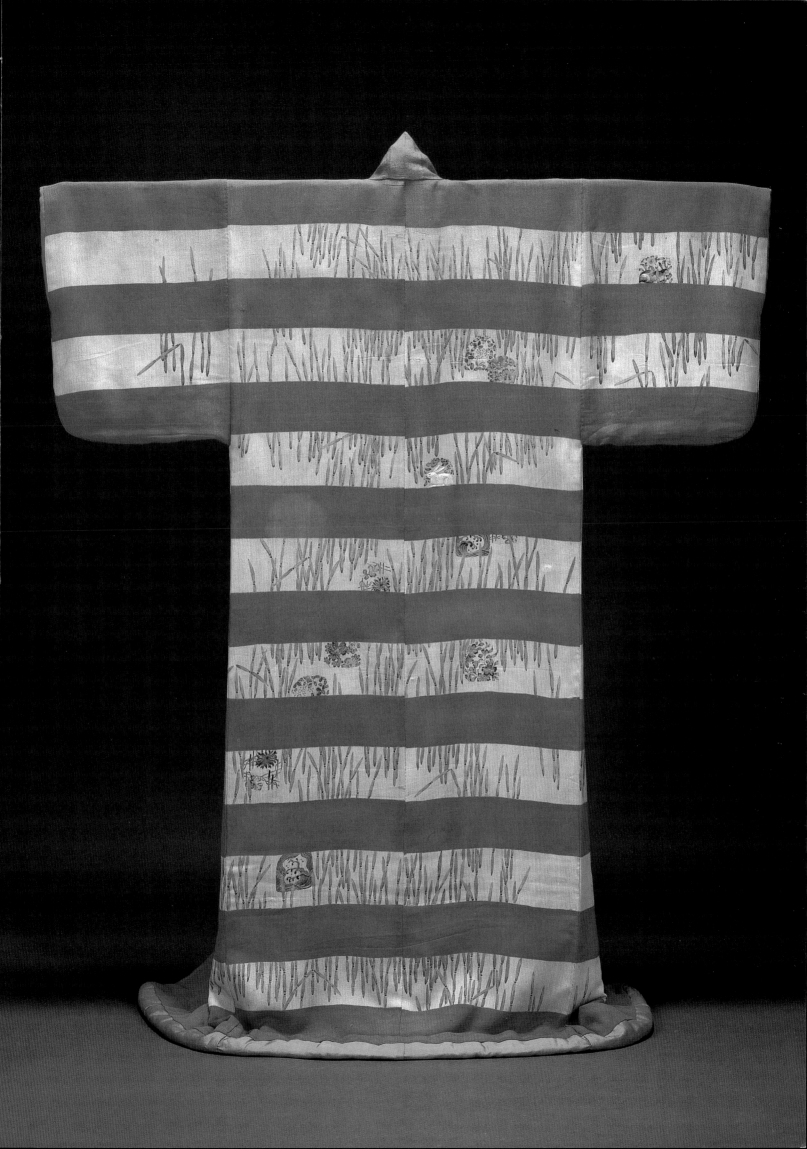

15

Kosode with Roses and Tortoise-
shell Grid
Yūzen dyeing and embroidery on
  light blue crepe (*chirimen*) ground
Silk
Edo period, 18th century

Spirals, roses, and tortoise-shell grids
(*kikkō tsunagi*, hexagonal grids) cascade
diagonally from the right shoulder
down to the left hem. The tortoise-shell
grids with three projections at the
corners, the roses, with their undulating
stems, and leaves are reserved in white
by means of paste-resist on the bright
blue ground (*shiroage*), and are hand
colored in complex color schemes with
some shadings. The tortoise-shell grid
pattern, also reserved in white by means
of paste-resist, creates a striking
contrast against the colored areas. The
vermilion in the roses is not painted,
but is supplemented by embroidery,
which adds a lustrous finish to the
already dyed surface. In *yūzen* dyeing,
embroidery was often used as an
effective supplement.

SK

Pl. 15

64

16

Furisode with Treasure Boats
Yūzen dyeing on dark-blue crepe
  (*chirimen*) ground
Silk
Edo period, 18th century

The *furisode* is a variation of the *kosode* with long swinging sleeves. They were worn by young girls and unmarried maidens. The decorative theme on this *furisode* is treasure boats sailing through a storm in rough ocean waves, as they return from abroad bringing countless treasures. As is often seen in *kosode* decorative compositions, the boats, rain, and waves are placed diagonally from the right shoulder to the left side of the skirt.

The sails, flags, and banners are densely filled with geometric and auspicious motifs—seven treasures, lozenges, rising serpentine lines, and hemp leaves, all of which are rendered by means of paste-resist dyeing and then colored by hand. The curving waves and diagonal lines representing the wind are reserved in white, with no added color.

The complex and delicate use of the white outlines around each motif and the hand coloring are typical *yūzen* techniques of the middle Edo period, when *yūzen* dyeing was at its peak of technical excellence. Here the prominent use of white reserve in the wind and waves suggests a slightly later date, probably the late Edo period.

SK

17

Uchikake (outer *kosode*) with
Shell-matching Game
Yūzen dyeing on dark-blue figured satin
  (*rinzu*) ground
Silk
Edo period, 18th century

The entire robe is decorated with
hexagonal shell buckets and painted
shells, representing the theme of the
shell-matching game. Beginning in the
Heian period, the game was popular
among court ladies. Two identical sets
of 180 clam shells were fashioned; each
pair of shells had a miniature painting
on the interior. The painting themes
were taken from famous poetry
anthologies or classical literature,
particularly the *Tale of Genji*, a novel of
the romantic life of the charming
prince Hikaru Genji and his son Kaoru,
written by Lady Murasaki (978–1015)
between years 1000 and 1010.

   The game is played somewhat like
the Western card game "Concentra-
tion." One set of shells was randomly
placed face down on the floor, while the
other set was shown one at a time, face
up. The players tried to find the
matching shell on the floor; the one
who matched the most pairs was the
winner. In time, this game came to
connote a union between man and
woman; thus it became an appropriate
motif for wedding robes, bedding,
furniture, and toiletry articles. It is not
clear, however, if this particular *kosode*
was used for a wedding ceremony. The
technical proficiency of *yūzen* dyeing in
this robe is obvious in the fine details of
the shells and shell buckets.

                                    SK

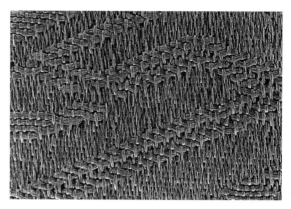

17. *Uchikake.* Figured satin *(rinzu)* of a five-harness, weft-faced
satin figure on five-harness, warp-faced satin ground. The
figure is the typical key fret with orchids and chrysanthemums
(rangiku). (Detail)

18

Katabira (summer *kosode*)
with Plums and Quivers
Yūzen dyeing on white ground
Ramie
Edo period, 18th century

The all-over decorative pattern of this *katabira* with plums and quivers is executed in fine *yūzen* dyeing and embroidery. The summery indigo blue on the plum trees is accentuated by the crimson, yellow, and light blue in the flowers. The quivers themselves are decorated with very fine motifs of hemp leaves, wickerwork fishnet, and vine scrolls (*karakusa*), again achieved by *yūzen* dyeing.

The combination of plum and quiver was derived from an episode related to the Battle of Ikuta no Mori in the *Genpei Seisui ki* (Rise and Fall of the Genji and the Heike Families), established in the Kamakura period (1185–1333). One of the great war romances of the middle Heian period (794–1185), it tells of the rise and decline of the Minamoto and Taira clans. Kajiwara Genta Kagesue departed for the battle carrying a blossoming plum branch in the quiver on his back. The Japanese were touched by this heartwarming indication that a fearless warrior possessed a tender heart; even in a life-or-death situation, he could appreciate the beautiful plum blossoms which had just opened in the early, still cold spring.

SK

18. *Katabira*. Plain-weave ramie ground shows a thin resist line *(itome)*, a characteristic of *yūzen* dyeing. (Detail)

Pl. 18

19

Katabira (summer *kosode*) with
  Tanabata Bamboo
Yūzen dyeing on white ground
Ramié
Edo period, 18th century

Delicate bamboo stems rise from the
skirt and spread their branches to both
shoulders. The bamboo branches are
decorated with Tanabata poem cards
and miniature lanterns, which are
gently blowing in the evening breeze.
Tanabata is celebrated annually on
July 7, to wish good luck the legendary
lovers living in the sky and exiled to
separate corners across the Milky Way,
who are allowed to meet only once a
year on this day. Even today the
Japanese decorate bamboo branches
with colorful trimmings to pray for a
lovely evening for the hero and heroine
of this story. *Hagi* (bush clover), a
plant of the fall, surrounds the bamboo
stems, suggesting the coming of
autumn.

    The excellent *yūzen* technique is
obvious in the delicate coloring,
especially in the *tarashikomi*, a painting
technique of blotting two colors while
they are wet.

                                        SK

20 *(following page)*

Furisode for a Male Child with
  Seven Good Luck Gods
Yūzen dyeing on blue crepe (*chirimen*)
  ground
Silk
Edo period, 18th century

Although *furisode* with their long
swinging sleeves are primarily worn
by girls and unmarried women, male
babies and toddlers may also wear
them. This *furisode* for a male child is
adorned with the Seven Gods of Good
Luck motif, rendered in the *yūzen*
dyeing technique: Daikoku, the god of
wealth; Ebisu, the god of daily food,
chiefly fish; Fukurokuju, the god of
longevity; Jurōin, the god of scholas-
tic success; Benten, the goddess of love
and music; and Bishamonten, the god
of worldly prosperity. Hotei, the god of
contentment and happiness, is missing.
His absence, however, is cleverly
calculated. The child himself is meant to
be this god.

    Children's garments were often
decorated with auspicious symbols,
reflecting their parents' ardent prayers
for their happiness, good health, and
success. The red stitching down the back
is called a back-guard, another symbol
of protection. The stitching patterns
were different for boys and girls; this
pattern of paired dots (.. .. ..) was
designated for a boy's robe.

                                        SK

21 *(following page)*

Furisode for a Female Child with
  Chrysanthemums
Yūzen dyeing on blue crepe ground
Silk
Edo period, 18th century

This *furisode* is charmingly decorated
with "thousands of chrysanthemums,"
one of the great favorites of Japanese
flowers, arranged in different pots and
vases. The back-guard stitching of
alternation dots and long lines on this
garment indicates this *furisode* was
for a girl.

                                        SK

Pl. 19

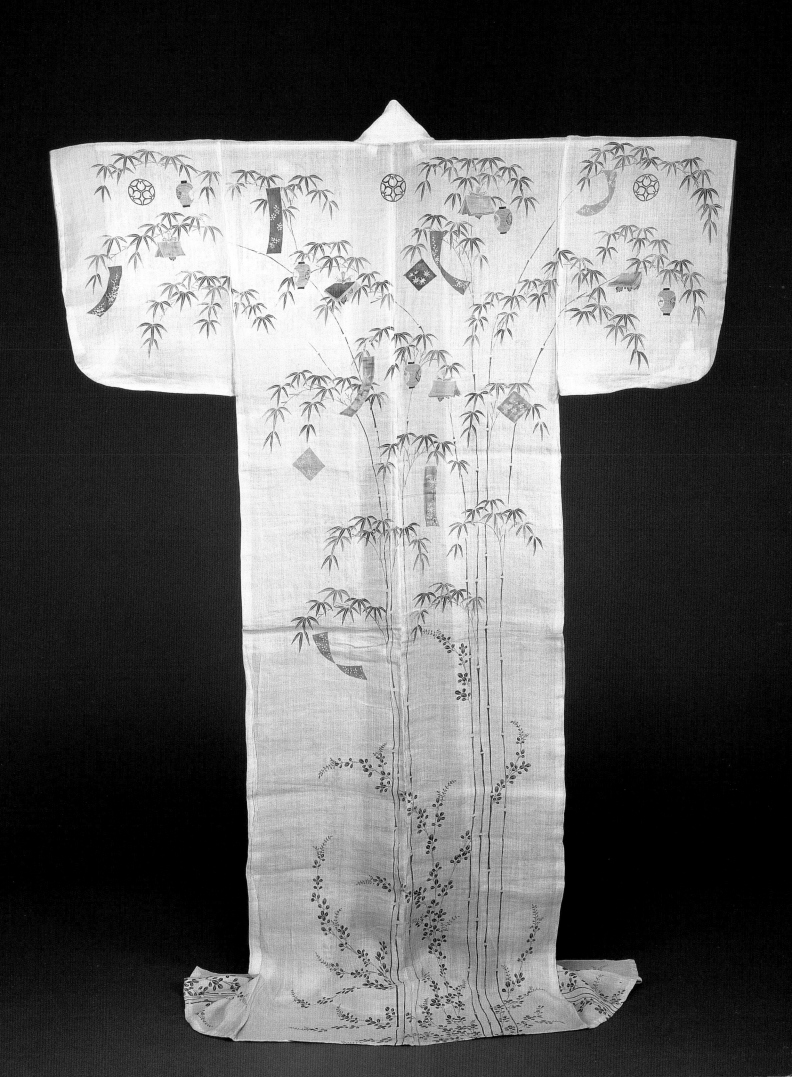

22

Uchikake (outer *kosode*) with Landscapes
  and Activities of the Four Seasons
Yūzen dyeing and embroidery on grey crepe
  (*chirimen*) ground
Silk
Edo-Meiji period, 19th century

On this *uchikake*, fans, umbrellas, and
human beings are depicted scattered among
landscape elements suggesting various
seasonal activities. The gentle elegance of
the design indicates that this robe was
executed in Kyoto-style *yūzen* dyeing. The
naturalistic depictions of the small motifs,
the somewhat dark, but refined color tone,
the occasional bright colors (which look
like chemical dyes), and the very fine
embroidery are all characteristics of the
period from the end of the Edo to the
beginning of the Meiji (1868–1911) period.
                                          SK

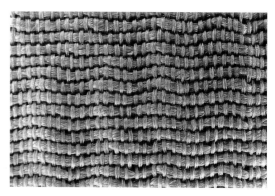

22. *Uchikake.* Silk crepe *(chirimen).* A kind of crepe made
by especially twisted weft threads *(kabe ito),* which create
more texture. (Detail)

Pl. 22

IMPERIAL ROBES

23

Ohiki Nōshi (long *nōshi*) with Triple
  Lozenge Diaper
Sha gauze of *kome* weave of reddish-blue
  ground
Silk
Edo period, 19th century

Long, trailing *nōshi* were everyday garments
for emperors and retired emperors. They
were worn by these men of the highest rank
for formal occasions during the Muromachi
period, but later came to be used for more
casual wear.

The cut is long; when worn, the
garment spreads in front and trails in back.
This particular *nōshi* was intended to be a
summer garment for Emperor Kōmei
(1831–66), but was completed in the fourth
month of 1867, four months after his early
death at age thirty-six, on the twenty-fifth
of the twelfth month of 1866. It is double
breasted, closes on the right side with a
knotted button, and has large sleeves with
wrist openings that extend the full width of
the sleeves *(ōsode)*. As is usual in summer
nōshi, it is unlined, made of *sha* gauze with
kome-weave patterning of triple lozenges
diaper *(miedasuki)* done by floating wefts.
The gauze weave makes a texture that
resembles grains lying in a row and thus is
called *kome* (rice) weave. The fabric was
dyed in a special dyeing technique, *futaai*,
where the threads were dyed twice, first in
blue and then in red. For younger men's
robes, the material was dyed with more
vermillion and less blue; as wearers got
older the red hue was reduced.

SK

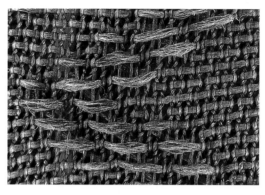

23-1. *Nōshi. Sha gauze* in *kome* weave. Warp ends are
made to cross over every weft in opposite directions,
causing the wefts to be slightly lifted. The wefts look like
rice grains lying in a row, creating a pattern called *kome*
(rice) weave. Weft-faced, float-woven figures are created
on this *kome* weave ground. (Detail)

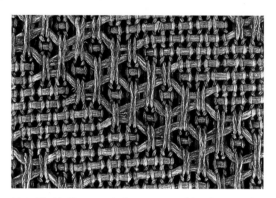

23-2. *Nōshi. Sha* gauze in *kome* weave. This robe is made
wrong-side out on purpose, as was sometimes done in
imperial robes in the Edo period. Here, as in 23-1, the
warp ends also cross over every weft, but the weft-faced,
float-woven figures look more intricate on this side of
fabric. (Detail)

Pl. 23

24

Ko-nōshi (informal *nōshi*) with
  Flying Cranes in White woven-pattern
  on light-blue ground
Sha gauze
Silk
Edo, 19th century

Ko-nōshi (short *nōshi*) are simpler in cut
than *nōshi* . From the Heian period on,
they were reserved for court nobles
ranked at or above the ministers and
commanders (*taishō*) of the Imperial
Bodyguard when they were on private
outings, but they were not worn for work
at the palace. *Ko-nōshi* are similar in
design to a *kariginu* (hunting jacket), an
everyday robe, but have a horizontal band
(*ran*) added all around the hem for a
dignified and sumptuous effect. Thus it is
ranked higher than *kariginu*.

    Double-breasted, with a round neck
and a stiff collar, this *ko-nōshi* has large
rectangular sleeves. The wrist opening
extends he full width of the sleeves, which
are decorated with draw-cords at the
outer edges. As a rule emperors did not
use *ko-nōshi*, but retired emperors and
princes wore them in place of *kariginu*.
This *ko-nōshi* was made in 1852 for Prince
Takahito, the eighth head of the
Arisugawa family. Made of *sha*, a stiff
gauze, it was the prince's summer robe.

                          SK

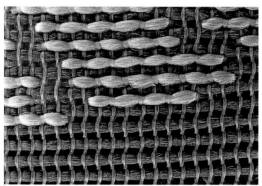

24. *Nōshi. Sha* gauze. Warp threads are made to cross over
the next warp in the same direction. The white woven
patterns are developed by introducing a complementary
weft thread where required. (Detail)

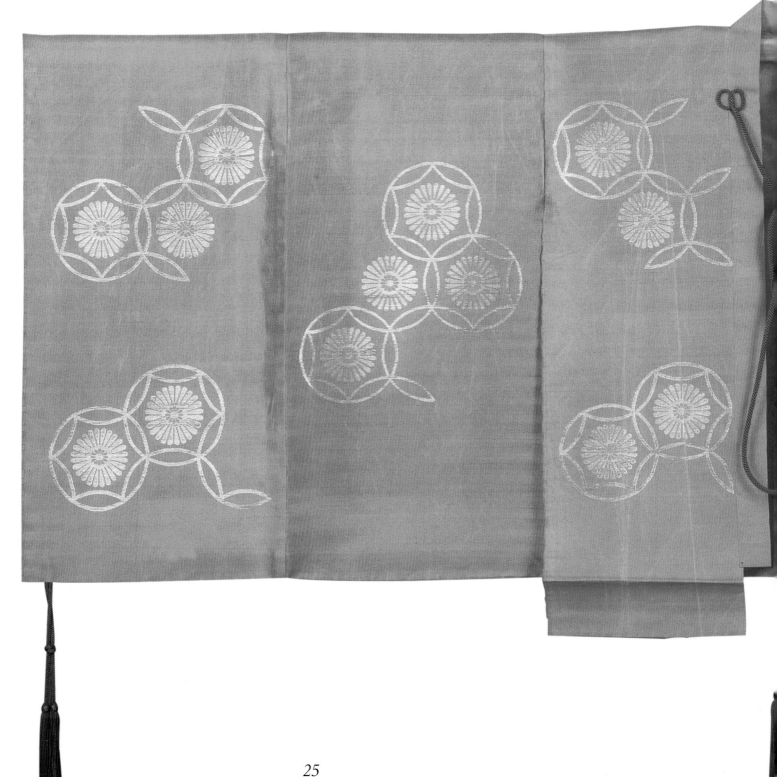

25

Mari Suikan (jacket for football)
  with Broken Circles Enclosing
  Chrysanthemums
Sha gauze in gold
Silk
Edo period, 19th century

Japanese football is played by eight men who kick a leather ball among the players without letting it hit the ground. The short jacket specified for this sport is called *mari suikan* (jacket for ball). Before the Edo period there was no such special jacket, but at the end of the Muromachi period, ballplayers in the court customarily wore *hitatare* of silk tacked under full trousers (*hakama*) made of *kuzu* fiber. The *hitatare* has a

Pl. 25

short, narrow body with a cord attached to the neckband, which goes around the chest and is looped across the front.

This *suikan*, similar to *hitatare* in cut, is decorated with a design of broken circles enclosing chrysanthemums on a peach-colored ground. Before it entered Prince Takamatsu's collection, it had been handed down in the Arisugawa family, a princely household established by a son of Emperor Go-Yozei (1571–1617). The inscription on the wrapping paper mentions that it was "newly made in the seventh month of 1813." The jacket was further referred to in the register of the Asukai family, generations of which coached football at the court: "This upper garment in peach color in gold brocade was made on July 19, 1813 for Prince Tsuguhito (1784–1845), the seventh head of the Arisugawa family."

SK

26

Trousers for Football with Leather
  Decoration
Light-red plain weave
Kuzu (kudzu vine) and cotton
Edo period, 19th century

These trousers for football are made of
kuzu (kudzu vine). The wide hem
borders of red silk contain drawcords,
which were pulled to close around the
ankle when the garment was worn.

Below the knees the trousers are
decorated with *kawatsuyu*, attachments
of leather, that derived from the braided
cord (*kikutoji*) once used to strengthen
the seams; later they came to serve only
a decorative function.

SK

27 (following page)

Nōshi (*warawa noshi*) with Hollyhocks
White floating pattern weave (*uki-orimono*)
Silk
Edo period, 19th century

This *nōshi* for a male child was made for
Prince Taruhito of the Arisugawa family
in the second month of 1849. *Warawa
nōshi* (lit. child's *nōshi*) was formal
attire for princes and young noblemen
before they assumed manhood. As a
rule, winter *nōshi* were in white with
small hollyhock patterns in float weave,
and were lined with purple silk of plain
weave. In general, *nōshi* for younger
men were decorated with smaller
patterns; older men tended to wear *nōshi*
with larger patterns. This robe is an
example of a small-patterned *nōshi* for a
young prince. The cut is similar to that
for an adult. *Nōshi* were worn with
sashinuki hakama (trousers, cat. no. 28).

SK

28 (following page)

Sashinuki Hakama (trousers) with
  Medallions Enclosing Butterflies and
  Woven tortoise-shell diaper (*kikkō*)
  on purple ground
Double weave (*futae-orimono*)
Silk
Edo period, 18th century

Sashinuki, a type of trousers, are pleated
both in front and back. When worn, the
drawcords close at the ankles, making
the trousers look voluminous at the
bottom. These trousers were worn by
Prince Yorihito of the Arisugawa family.
Sashinuki for young princes were
always made with woven designs
executed in relief in white circles
containing four butterflies, each facing
the center and spreading their wings on
a purple ground with tortoise-shell
diapers.

SK

26. *Hakama* for football. Plain weave of
cotton warp threads cross the kudzu-vine
weft threads. (Detail)

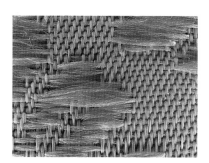

27. *Nōshi* for male child. Twill weave *(aya-ori)*.
Weft-faced, float woven figures are developed on
warp-faced twill ground. (Detail)

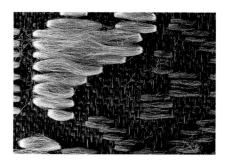

28. *Sashinuki* trousers. Twill weave *(aya-ori)*. Weft-
faced, float-woven figure of tortoise-shell diaper on
warp-faced twill ground, with additional pattern of
circles containing butterflies developed by introducing a complementary weft. (Detail)

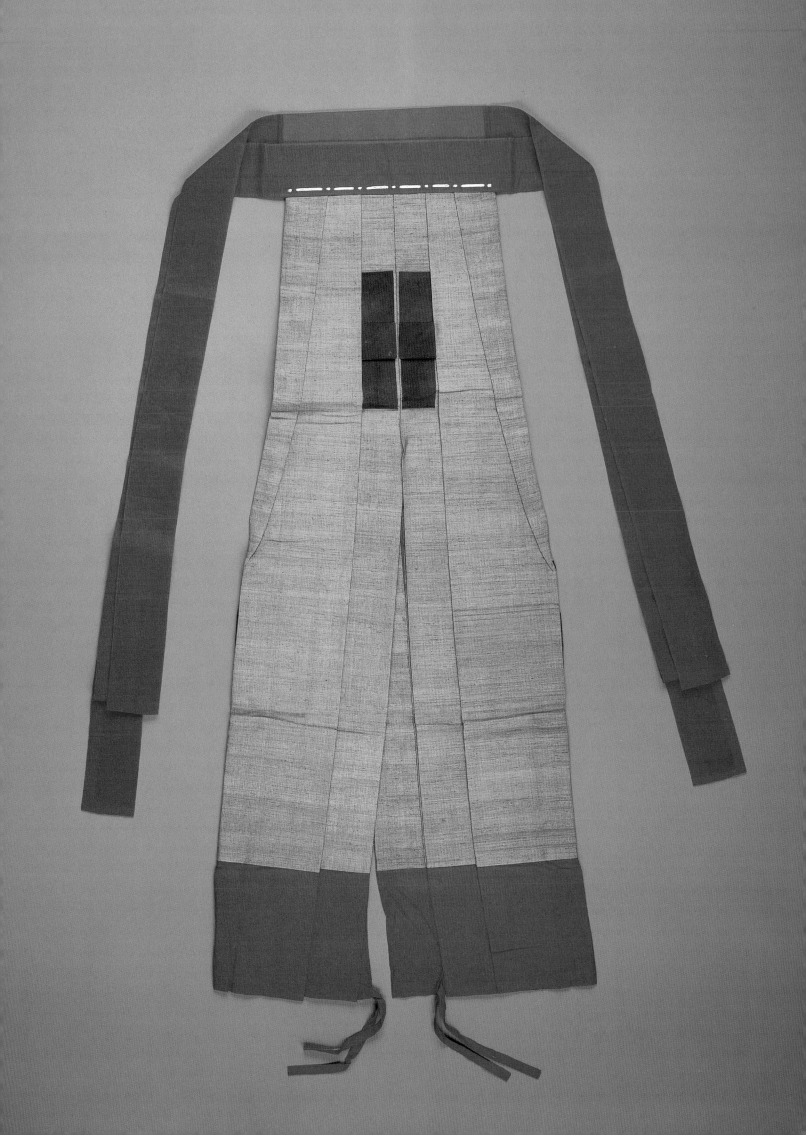

Pl. 27

Pl. 28

29

Hanjiri (jacket for a young prince) with
  Opposed Vertical Serpentine Lines
  (tatewaku) Enclosing Wisteria
Golden-yellow *sha* gauze
Silk
Edo period, 19th century

The *hanjiri* (lit. jacket with short back panel), a garment for a male child, was used for formal occasions such as Fukasogi, a ceremony in which the child's hair was trimmed to pray for good health and long hair. In cut it is similar to the *kariginu* (hunting jacket) in that it is double breasted with a round neck and short neckband, but it has a short back panel, hence the name "short back." The large sleeves are decorated with cords made of a chain of chrysanthemums on the outer edges. The jacket was worn with a belt of the same material as the jacket.

This *hanjiri* was in the possession of the Arisugawa family before it entered Prince Takamatsu's collection. It is a summer cloth in stiff *sha* gauze the color of the *yamabuki*, or yellow rose (*Kerria japonica*), which makes a beautiful contrast with the vermilion lining.

SK

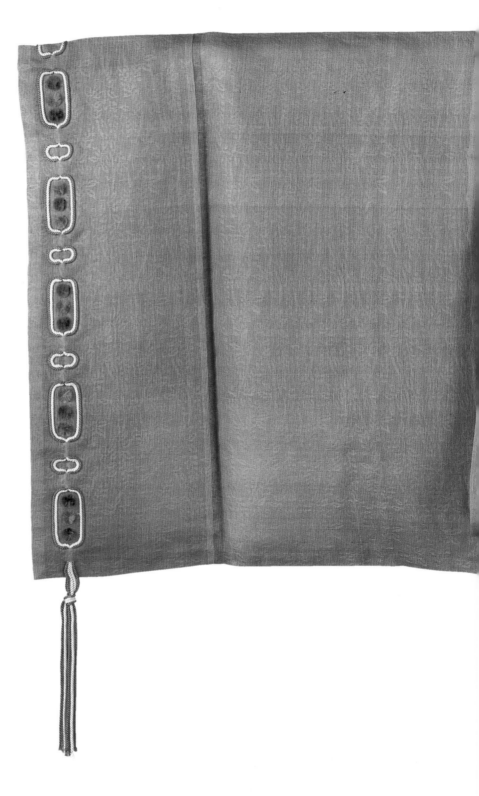

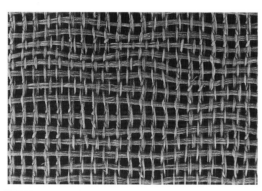

29. *Hanjiri.* Patterned *sha* gauze. Sets of three warps are made to cross, making an open mesh. The pattern is created by plain weave; the open mesh in the gauze weave makes the plain-weave areas look patterned. (Detail)

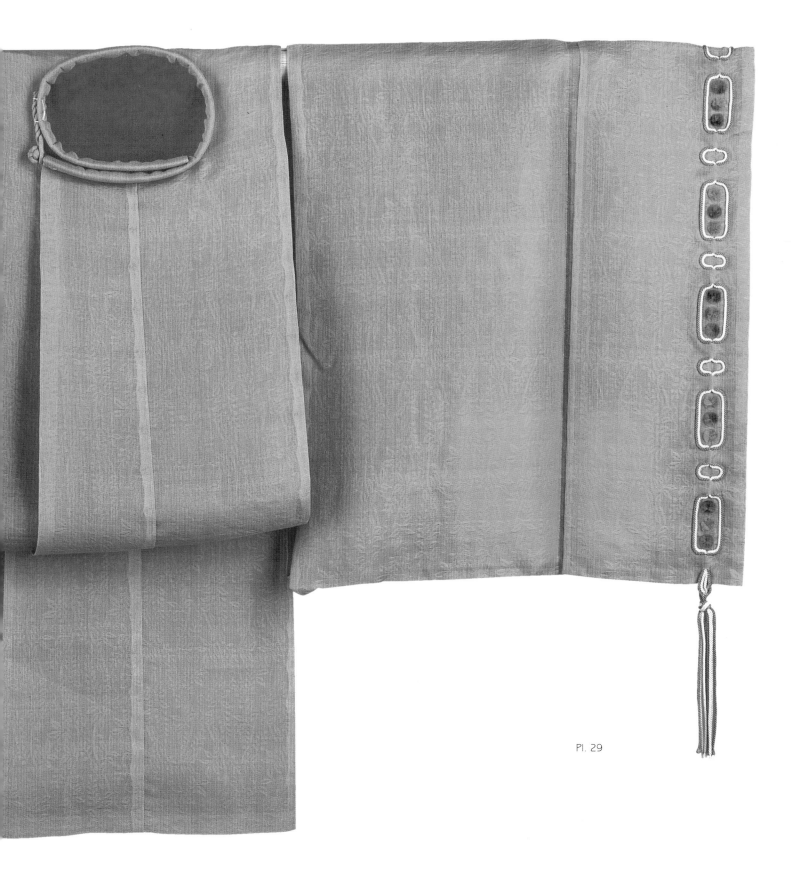

Pl. 29

30

Hosonaga (young princess's robe) with Pine Lozenges and Light-blue Tortoise-shell Interlocking pattern on green ground
Double weave *(futae orimono)*
Silk
Edo period, 19th century

Hosonaga (lit. narrow and long robe) were worn by young princes on occasions such as the Fukasogi ceremony, when a child's hair was trimmed to pray for good hair growth. As the name denotes, *hosonaga* are usually long in cut, but this example is not so long in comparison to other garments of this type.

This *hosonaga* has a white woven pattern (double weave) of pines in lozenges on a light-blue, tortoise-shell interlocking pattern. The green ground color beautifully contrasts with the purple of the lining. Since a *hosonaga* of the same color combination is known to have been worn by Princess Kazu (Kazu no Miya) for her Fukasogi ceremony in 1851, this robe was very likely worn by a girl of high birth for a similar ceremony.

SK

31 *(following page)*

Kosode with Willow and Cherry Blossoms
Embroidery on vermilion crepe *(chirimen)* ground
Silk
Edo period, 18th century

This *kosode* is decorated with cherry blossoms scattered over a latticework of willow branches. Reflecting an eighteenth-century fashion trend, the composition is emphasized on the right side of the back; the decorative motifs cascade down from the right shoulder to the left hem, leaving an empty area on the left waist.

The light green of the willows and the pink of the blossoms on a vermilion ground make a beautiful contrast. It alludes to a spring scene in Kyoto as described by the priest-poet Sosei, of the early Heian period:

Miwatase ba	Look all around—
yanagi sakura o	patches of
kokimaze te	willows and cherry.
Miyako zo haru no	Kyoto looks like a
nishiki nari keri	brocade of spring.

This elegant literary theme was brilliantly expressed in embroidery alone. Ladies in the court wore robes painstakingly embroidered, as they considered dyeing an inexpensive version of embroidery.

SK

32 *(following page)*

Furisode with Wisteria and Flying Cranes
Embroidery on vermilion crepe *(chirimen)* ground
Silk
Edo period, 19th century

On the vermilion crepe ground, this *furisode* was embroidered with clusters of wisteria and cranes, expressing typical Japanese taste. The spacing of the undulating vines and flowers of the wisteria and the freely flying cranes among them is well calculated for excellent balance. This graceful *furisode* was most likely used by a young daughter of a court noble.

SK

Pl. 30

33

Katabira with Cherry Blossoms, Flowing
  Streams, Reeds, and Herons
Dyeing and embroidery on light-black
  ground
Ramie
Edo period, 19th century

The crescent moon done in embroidery
suggests that the pale black ground was
meant to express the night. The cherry
blossoms and the waves are rendered by
shiroage (lit. depiction in white) paste-resist
in white, and the herons and flowers are
depicted by supplementary embroidery. The
combination of cherry blossoming in the
night and herons is unusual in robe design.

    The sophisticated design, restrained
dignity, and gentle grace suggest that this
katabira was worn by a lady-in-waiting of
the imperial court.

                       SK

Pl. 33

96

SAMURAI CLASS ROBES

34

Kosode with Chrysanthemums
   and the Poem *Kimi ga yo*
Dyeing and embroidery on white-figured satin
   (rinzu) ground
Silk
Edo period, 19th century

This *kosode* was probably worn by a lady-
in-waiting in service to a daimyo. It was
customary that the robes of such women
were decorated with auspicious motifs,
often congratulatory poems. In this
kosode, longevity symbols rise from the
hem to the shoulders along graceful
stems of chrysanthemums, and the
characters of a congratulatory poem
from *Wakan rōeishū* (Anthology of
Japanese and Chinese Poems; compiled
around 1011–1012) are scattered over the
flowers on the upper part of the back.
Written by an unknown author, the
poem is now widely known as *Kimi ga yo*
(His Majesty's Reign) and is identified as
the Japanese national anthem, although it
has never been officially adopted.

Kimi ga yo wa	Reign a
	thousand years
Chiyo ni yachiyo ni	My lord, until
Sazare ishi no	What are pebbles
	now
Iwao to narite	By age united to
	mighty rocks
Koke no musu	shall grow moss
made	on their sides

SK

35 *(following page)*

Uchikake with Bamboo Blinds,
   Wisteria, and Peonies
Dyeing and embroidery on white-figured
   satin *(rinzu)* ground
Silk
Edo period, 19th century

The *uchikake* was worn by women of
the samurai as well as those of the
merchant class. On the shiny, white,
figured ground, the decorative motif of
bamboo blinds are shown rolled and
unrolled. The blinds are decorated with
peonies and wisteria flowers executed
with a brush and embroidery, together
with stenciled "fawn spot" patterns
called *suri hitta*, an imitation of *kanoko*
tie-dyeing.
   The *suri hitta* patterns appeared as
the result of the feudal government's
banning of expensively decorated
robes. The technique was able to
produce the visual effect but not the
texture of the finely knotted tie-dyed
kanoko technique.
   During the Edo period, bamboo
screens were considered a reminder of
the good old days of the Heian period,
and thus were appropriate auspicious
motifs for a woman's garment.

SK

36 *(following page)*

Hitoe (unlined *kosode*) with
   Goshodoki Design
Dyeing and embroidery on light-blue
   crepe *(chirimen)* ground
Silk
Edo period, 19th century

This unlined *kosode* (*hitoe*) was a gift to
a lady-in-waiting in service to the Kishū
branch family of the Tokugawa Shogun.
Because the kimono was a gift from her
lord, the recipient was allowed to use
the *mon* (family crest) of her lord on
that attire. She would have been very
proud of it throughout her life.
   The entire lower portion, below
obi level, is decorated with typical
goshodoki motifs executed by fine
dyeing and embroidery. The goshodoki
design typically appeared on *kosode* of
women of high samurai class in the late
Edo period. Literally translated as
"clearing up the imperial themes," this
design derived from natural scenes of
the gardens of the imperial palace in
Kyoto. The motifs often incorporated
scenes and objects taken from classical
literature, particularly from Heian
poetry and stories and Noh plays. In
this *hitoe*, the *goshodoki* motif is
supplemented with flowers of the four
seasons, palaces and pavilions, flowing
streams, imperial carriages, garden
fences, and fans. By the end of the Edo
period the symbolic meaning had
become diluted, and the motifs were
highly stylized.
   The design in this *hitoe* reveals the
samurai-class women's high standards
and taste for classics. (Only in the later
Edo period did such designs come to be
called *goshodoki*). The *hitoe*'s original
stitching is still intact, an additional
asset of the robe.

SK

Pl. 34

37

Katabira (summer *kosode*) with
  Yatsuhashi Bridges and Irises
Dyeing and embroidery on
  white ground
Ramié
Edo period, 19th century

The design concentrated in the lower part
of the *kosode* and the family crest of the
three-leaved hollyhock suggest that this
katabira was a gift to a lady-in-waiting
from her lord, probably one of the
Tokugawa branch families.

 The combined decorative motifs of
irises and Yatsuhashi bridges allude to the
ninth chapter of the *Tales of Ise*, "*Mikawa
no kuni Yatsuhashi*" (Yatsuhashi Bridges of
the Mikawa Province,) where Ariwara no
Narihira rested on his way to the eastern
provinces.

 The robes of ladies-in-waiting were
often decorated with literary themes of the
Heian period. The flying swallows give a
feeling of spring to the decoration.

SK

38 *(following page)*

Furisode for Female Child with Rocks,
  Flowing Streams, and Azalea
Dyeing and embroidery on light-blue
  crepe (*chirimen*) ground
Silk
Edo period, 19th century
Tamura Shizuko Collection

The azaleas blossoming near streams
are rendered in white reserve by paste-
resist dyeing and embroidery. The
design composition is concentrated
around the hem, and a smaller number
of azalea flowers are scattered on both
sleeves in well-planned spacing.

 During the nineteenth century, the
decorative composition tended to
concentrate on the lower part of the
robe. This child's *furisode*, a *kosode* with
long sleeves, attests that children's robes
followed the same trend.

 From the family crest (*mon*) of the
water plantain (*omodaka*), this *furisode*
is identified as the attire of a daughter
of the lord of the Mori clan in Suō and
Nagato provinces (present-day
Yamaguchi prefecture). The tucks on
both shoulders (*kataage*) are to adjust
the shoulder width to the child. As she
grew, these tucks were let out and
became smaller.

SK

39 *(following page)*

Hitoe Furisode (baby's summer robe)
  with *Goshodoki* Design
Dyeing and embroidery on light-green
  ground
Ro gauze
Silk
Edo period, 19th century

This unlined (*hitoe*) *furisode* is decorated with a landscape of flowers, rocks,
and streams in paste-resist white and
embroidery. Landscape designs with
flowers, grasses, and objects alluding to
literary subjects were called *goshodoki*
(clearing up the imperial themes). Such
motifs were popular among the women
of the high-ranking samurai class. It
reveals their nostalgic view of imperial
life and an aspiration to master the
classical literature and Noh plays of the
Heian period.

 In this *furisode*, peonies and a lion
are rendered in addition to the
landscape elements. These motifs
allude to the Noh play *Shakkyō* (Stone
Bridge), which tells of the Buddhist
monk Jakusho's journey to Tang China,
where he traveled to the holy mountain
of Seiryōzan and came upon a lion
dancing. This baby's *furisode* demon-
strates that the *goshodoki* motif was
popular on children's robes as well as
those of adults. The "back guard," done
in green stitching on the back of the
robe, is a symbolic guard to assure the
child's good health and undisturbed
growth.

SK

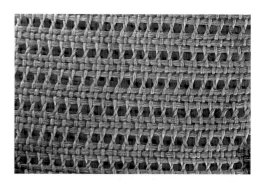

39. *Furisode.* A type of gauze called *ro*, made by a
combination of plain and gauze weaves. Every three
wefts, the warp ends are made to cross over other
warp ends. *Ro* is softer than *sha* gauze. (Detail)

Pl. 37

Pl. 38

106

Pl. 39

40

Koshimaki (waist wrap) with Myriad
  Treasures, Pine, Bamboo, and Plums
Dyeing and embroidery on reddish black
  ground
Silk
Edo period, 19th century

During the hot, humid summer in
Japan, to dress comfortably yet properly
was a challenge for women of the
highest status of the samurai class. In
the middle of the Muromachi period
(1392–1573), *uchikake* (outer *kosode*)
were tied at the waist, slipped off the
shoulders, and draped from the waist.
During the seventeenth century, special
outer garments called *koshimaki* (lit.
waist wrap) replaced the heavy
uchikake, and in the eighteenth century,
another special style of dress developed.
Koshimaki were worn over *katabira*
slipped off the shoulders and arms. The
obi was wrapped around the waist over
the *koshimaki*, and its stiff ends were
extended through the sleeves to hold
them out to either side.

　　Koshimaki were made of plain silk
dyed dark brown or black and embroidered with small repeated patterns of
auspicious symbols.

　　This example was embroidered
with the myriad treasures motif,
(*takarazukushi*), symbols of material
prosperity and good fortune, together
with the Three Friends of Winter,
pines, bamboos, and plum, which are
symbols of longevity, resilience, and
purity respectively.

　　The assemblage of the myriad
treasures varies, but this *koshimaki*
includes:

　The hat and cape of invisibility
　The keys to the storehouse of
　　good fortune
　The flaming, wish-granting jewel
　The mallet of good fortune
　The money pouch
　Crossed cloves (sometimes identified as
　　rhinoceros horn)
　The seven jewels of gold, silver, and a
　　varying list of gemstones.

　　　　　　　　SK

PI. 41

PI. 42

41

Kakeshita Obi (sash used under the *uchikake*) with Peonies and Peacock Feathers
Embroidery on red velvet ground
Silk
Edo period, 19th century

This *obi* was worn by a woman of the samurai class around the waist of a *kosode* over which she wore an *uchikake* (formal outer garment). The name *kakeshita obi* (*obi* underneath *uchikake*) derived from this style of wearing *obi* and *uchikake*. Ladies-in-waiting in service to a *daimyō* tied the *obi* in front, and in winter warmed their hands by putting them into the knot. Embroidered in thick threads, and interfaced with layers of Japanese paper, this *obi* gives a powerful sculptural impression.

SK

42

Kakeshita Obi (sash used under the *uchikake*) with Bamboo and Tiger
Embroidery on purple satin ground
Silk
Edo period, 19th century

A lady-in-waiting in service to a daimyo used this *obi* over a *kosode* and under an *uchikake*. In many cases this kind of *obi* was made of heavy materials such as satin and velvet, and embroidered with bold designs. This satin *obi* is embroidered with tigers and bamboo, an unusual design for *obi*, although the tiger and bamboo theme appeared frequently in paintings.

SK

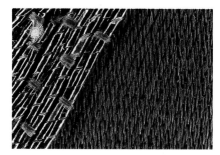

42. *Kakeshita-obi.* A fine-harness, warp-faced satin *(shusu)* supplemented with embroidery of nonstitchable gold threads. Two parallel threads are couched with a fine thread; four parallel threads are couched with a red thread. (Detail)

43

Hakoseko with Winter Plum Blossoms
Embroidery on light-blue velvet ground
Silk
Edo period, 19th century

Small box-shaped purses containing women's personal items, such as mirrors, combs, and tissue paper, was called *hakoseko*, and they were used by ladies-in-waiting in service to a daimyo. They were carried in the overlap in front above the *obi*. It is still used as an accessory for formal attire, such as wedding kimono.

During the later Edo period, *hakoseko* became a luxurious fashionable item. They were commonly made of heavy tapestry (*tsuzureori*), or appliquéd with imported felts, or heavily embroidered with gold thread. This *hakoseko* is decorated with plum blossoms, an early spring flower, expressing purity above the vulgar concerns of the mundane life.

SK

44

Hakoseko with Carp
Embroidery on reddish-brown velvet
    ground
Silk
Edo period, 19th century

This *hakoseko* is decorated with a carp,
an auspicious fish that guarantees
success and prosperity. Based on the
Chinese legend of Tōryūmon, a carp
that could leap over the Lungmen rapid
at of the Yellow River would become a
dragon.

   The carp is one of the most
popular symbols of courage and
strength.

SK

45

Tobacco Pouch with Peony
Slit tapestry (*tsuzure*) weave
Silk
Edo period, 19th century

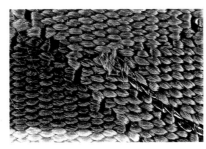

45. Tobacco pouch. Silk tapestry *(tsuzure-ori)* weave. Where colored areas meet, the weft threads are turned back around adjacent warp ends. If the juncture runs in the warp direction, a slit *(hatsuri)* in the fabric results. (Detail)

46

Tobacco Pouch with Bamboo
Slit tapestry (*tsuzure*) weave
Silk
Edo period, 19th century

Tobacco smoking was introduced into
Japan by Dutch traders during the early
seventeenth century, and the habit quickly
spread throughout Japanese society
because it was believed to be a panacea for
many illnesses. Ladies-in-waiting in
service, if they smoked, loved tobacco
pouches made of beautiful materials, such
as tapestry-weave silks and velvets.

   These tobacco pouches are connected
with the pipe cases by silver chains. The set
was carried by inserting the pipe case
between the folds of the *obi*. *Tsuzure* weave
is a plain weave with a design done in
colored wefts which are introduced where
required. Each color is interlaced with
warps only where that particular color is
required for the design.

SK

Pl. 43

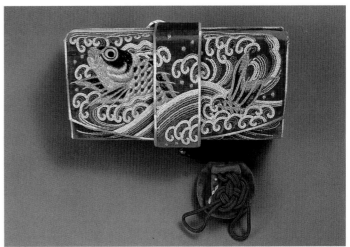

Pl. 44

Pl. 45

Pl. 46

TOILETRY ARTICLES
& WEDDING ROBES

Toiletry articles

Toiletry articles were intimately and importantly related to Japanese women's lives in many periods of Japan's history, but particularly during the Edo period, when elaborate makeup and hairstyles developed to match the splendor of *kosode* fashions. Brides of high status or wealth took to their new houses bridal trousseaus of lacquerware luxuriously decorated with sprinklings of gold (*maki-e*). The content of the trousseau commonly included three sets of shelves, boxes for personal use to be placed on these shelves, and various cosmetic paraphernalia.

47
Toiletry Set with Plum and Cherry
 Blossoms
Maki-e on lacquered wood
Edo period, 17th century

A mirror stand is a major piece in a toiletry set. A circular bronze mirror is held on two posts that rise from a square or rectangular box with drawers. In the drawers are stored the mirror, combs, a hair oil holder, and equipment for tooth blackening (*ohaguro*).

The entire surface of the stand is decorated with *maki-e*, a lacquering technique uniquely Japanese, in which gold flakes or powders are sprinkled on the lacquered surface while it was still wet. The decorative motifs used here are blossoming plum and cherry, the most favored flowers in Japan. The small objects inside the drawers were decorated with the same motifs that adorned the mirror stand in *maki-e* technique. The metal utensils are incised with the crest of paulownia, the family crest of the owner. The objects are examples of lacquered cosmetic wares from the early Edo period.

AH

Pl. 47

48

Covered, Red-cornered Box with Yellow
  Roses and Flowing Water

Maki-e on lacquered wood

Edo period, 17th century

Cosmetic boxes were already in use during
the Heian period (794–1192), and during
the medieval period they were treated as
sacred objects to be dedicated to Shinto
shrines.

    This lidded box was made in red
lacquer and *maki-e* to contain cosmetics
and other personal articles for a new bride.
Originally from a pair consisting of one
large and one small box, this large box was
a part of a bridal trousseau. The decorative
motifs, yellow roses and gold-colored
flowers, were each chosen as an auspicious
symbol of prosperity and wealth.

AH

Pl. 48

49

Towel Stand with Arabesque and Three-
  leaved Hollyhock Crest

Maki-e on lacquered wood

Edo period, 18th century

Over a beautiful wood grain, this towel
stand is decorated with distinctively
Japanese plants—pine, bamboo, and plum,
the so-called Three Friends symbolic of
longevity, and the background is filled with
spirals executed in the *maki-e* technique.
The addition of the three-leaved hollyhock
crests indicates that this stand belonged to
a woman related to the Tokugawa family.

AH

Pl. 49

50

Ohaguro Set with Peony and Arabesque
Maki-e on lacquered wood, and gilt bronze
Edo period, 19th century

This set consists of a long rectangular box for storing the various utensils used in blackening teeth: a long, narrow gilt-bronze plate called *watashikane* (lit. metal to stretch across), which is placed across the rim of the basin with ear-shaped handles; a spouted ewer and a metal bowl to dissolve the stain; and a peacock feather used to apply the stain to the teeth. The basin is for rinsing the mouth, and the lidded square box stored the *haguro* powder that stained the teeth.

This peculiar custom of blackening teeth was practiced by men and women during the Heian period; in the Edo period, only married women followed this custom. The black stain was made of iron oxide. To ensure adherence of this liquid to the teeth, it was mixed with *fushiko*, a light-gray powder made from galls created by parasites (*Melaphis chinensis*) on trees whose wood contained tannin (such as oaks).

Except for metal objects, the entire surface of the pieces was decorated with peonies and arabesques in *maki-e*.

AH

Pl. 50

Pl. 51

PI. 52

51

Fusego with Peonies and Arabesque
Maki-e on lacquered wood
Edo period, 17th century
Tamura Shizuko Collection

Perfuming gives a final touch to dressing. The *fusego* (lit. basket to cover) was a device to perfume garments with incense. The garment was draped over the collapsible, mesh-covered box containing an incense burner. The *fusego* is decorated with chrysanthemum crests and sparrow crests, an indication of the two families involved. The sparrow crests suggest a daimyo family, while chrysanthemum crests indicate a noble court family. This *fusego* was very likely a trousseau piece of a daughter of a daimyo family who married a court noble.

AH

52

Melon-shaped Incense Burner with
   Metal Latticework
Maki-e on lacquered wood
Momoyama period, 16th century

Incense burners were an important household item in Japan, used for perfuming garments and to fill the rooms of the house with fragrance. In order to perfume garments, a burner was placed in a *fusego* (cat. no. 51), a collapsible, mesh-covered box over which a garment was draped.

AH

53

Head Rest (Incense Pillow) with Family Crests of Cranes in Circles

Maki-e on lacquered wood
Edo period, 18th century

An incense pillow is a special headrest used for perfuming the hair. On the short side, there is a drawer for storing incense; from the openings on the top and the long side rose the fumes from the burning incense. It is decorated with cranes in circles on a lacquered ground with gold dust sprinkled in patches (*muranashiji*). Because of the crests of cranes in circles, this pillow is considered to be one of the toilet objects prepared for the marriage of a daughter of the Nanbu family, the daimyo of the Morioka domain in present-day Iwate prefecture.

AH

Pl. 53

54

Melon-shaped Incense Burner

Maki-e on lacquered wood
Edo period, 17th century

The melon-shaped incense burner is decorated with circles containing cherry blossoms, pinks, gentian, mandarin oranges, and chrysanthemums. The burner is lined inside with a copper plate to make it fireproof and to hold the ashes, and is covered by a metal latticework. These circles are simply decorative motifs rather than family crests.

AH

Pl. 54

Pl. 55

Pl. 56

55
Toiletry Objects with Various Motifs
Copper and coral
Edo period, 19th century

This set consists of three cosmetic items: a lip brush, a face-powder brush, and a lip-rouge plate—a metal plate on which rouge was prepared for use by dissolving it with a bit of water. The plate is folded in half for carrying. The handles of the brushes and the rouge plate are all decorated with motifs of plum, cherry, maples, and ginko leaves.

SK

56
Toiletry Objects with Sword Motifs
Natural fiber, bronze
Edo period, 19th century

This set consists of a lip-rouge plate, lip brush, and face-powder brush with shapes deriving from sword decorations. The lip-rouge plate was shaped like a *tsuba* (sword guard), the lip-brush handle like a *kogai*, and the powder-brush handle in *tsukagashira* (a ferrule at the outer end of the hilt).

SK

57
Cosmetic Pouch with Ōhara Women and Maple Leaves
Tapestry weave
Silk
Edo period, 19th century

This handy pouch for carrying cosmetic objects is made of tapestry-weave silk with depictions of Ōhara women and maple leaves in changing colors, both Kyoto-derived motifs.

The pouch contains a rectangular mirror with chrysanthemums and a character of *kotobuki* (long life), a tortoise-shell comb, a powder brush with bell flowers, a rouge container, a brush, and a flat brush. Each piece was lacquered in Aizu province. Also included is a package of face powder with a picture of a woman represented in *ukiyo-e* style.

SK

Pl. 57

58

Wedding *Uchikake* (outer *kosode*)
  with Flying Cranes
Kanoko tie-dyeing on particolored,
  figured satin *(rinzu)* ground
Silk
Edo period, 19th century

All-over *kanoko* tie-dyeing (or *sō hitta shibori*) came into vogue in the latter half of the Edo period. This *uchikake*, used for a wedding, is spectacularly decorated with all-over *kanoko* tie-dyeing.

This *uchikake* is divided horizontally into three colored bands, with the shoulders and the hem areas in vermilion, and the waist to the lower portion of the sleeves in light brown. In this wide middle band, flying cranes are depicted by tie-dyeing in reserved color. The rest of the robe areas are filled with evenly tied *kanoko*.

Wedding robes decorated entirely with *kanoko* tie-dyeing seem to have been in vogue as early as the Genroku period (1688–1704). Ihara Saikaku (1642–1693), an acclaimed novelist, told a story of a rich bride who acquired several *kanoko* tie-dyed wedding robes in different colors. Even in the twentieth century, kimono in *kanoko* tie-dyeing are produced. The production process is extremely time-consuming and requires great mastery; only kimono of the best quality are done in the *so hitta shibori* technique.

In the late Edo period, the sleeves of robes became twice as long as in earlier times. Decorated with flying cranes, a symbol of longevity, this expensive *uchikake* was most appropriate for an extravagant wedding.

SK

59 *(following pages)*

Two Wedding *Uchikake* (Outer
  kosode) Decorated with *Noshi* and
  Paulownias
Tie-dyeing and embroidery on white
  figured satin *(rinzu)* ground
Tie-dyeing and embroidery on red-
  figured satin *(rinzu)* ground
Silk
Edo period, 19th century

Originally this set contained three *uchikake;* the third one was black. The bride wore all three *uchikake* at once.

These two *uchikake* are identical in design, with *noshi* and paulownia. *Noshi* are flattened, dried abalone strips which are decoratively bound with a cord. Because *noshi* sounds like the Japanese word for "expand" or "progress," dried strips of abalone came to be an auspicious symbol of the continuation of the family line. Paulownia (*kiri*) trees are the only nest of the phoenix, a mythical bird representing peace, prosperity, and enlightened rule. Because of their symbolic meaning and beautiful shape, the paulownia became one of the most favored plants of the Japanese. The two decorative motifs often appeared in wedding robes, bedding, and furniture.

The phoenix with widely spread wings, which appears on the white robe in embroidery, was an addition done in 1953. Perhaps it was intended to reinforce the symbolism of the paulownia and the phoenix.

SK

60

Wedding *Uchikake* (outer *kosode*) with
 Bamboo Blinds and Hollyhocks
Dyeing and embroidery on light-blue, plain-
 weave ground
Silk
Edo period, 19th century

This wedding *uchikake* was worn by a
woman of the samurai class in the late Edo
period. On plain-weave, light-blue silk,
decorative motifs of bamboo blinds and
hollyhock were executed by paste-resist
suri-hitta (a printed imitation of *kanoko*
tie-dyeing) and embroidery.

  On the upper areas of the back and
front are the embroidered black characters
of a poem from *Shūi Wakashū* (Collection
of Waka Gleanings; pub. between 1005–
1007). It is a congratulatory poem composed by Onakatomi no Yorimoto,
"Celebration at the Imperial Palace" in 934:

Hitofushi ni	One segment of this
chiyo o kometaru	bamboo cane contains
tsue nara ba	a thousand years
Tsuku tomo tsukiji	It will last forever
Kimi ga	Your Highness, like
yowai ha	your long life

There are indications that this *uchikake*
once had long sleeves, and sometime later
they were shortened to the present length.
The *uchikake* possesses a classical elegance
from the depiction of the poem and
bamboo blinds. This motif derived from
the life of Heian court nobles.

                                    SK

Pl. 60

HAIR
FASHION
TRENDS

Representative Hairstyles in the Edo Period

The eleven hair models presented here were reproduced in the twentieth century in half scale, based on paintings, drawings, and prints. These coiffures were popular in the Kyoto-Osaka region during the Edo period (17th–19th centuries).

Early Edo to Mid-Edo periods (17th to first half of the 18th century)

From the Heian to the Muromachi periods, Japanese women wore long hair, untied and trailing down the back. The fashion of tying hair began in the Momoyama and early Edo periods among Kabuki actresses and women in the pleasure quarters. The early tied style was simple—hair was tied in one knot at the top of the head, as seen in the Karawa style (Chinese ring; cat. no. 61). Characteristic of the mature phase of Japanese tied-hair style during the Edo period was that the hair was divided into four major sections: forelock (*maegami*), side locks (*bin*), back hair (*tsuto* or *tabo*), and topknot (*mage*). First the back hair was tied to make a puff around the lower back of the head. Next, the side locks were tied to make them protrude, and the forelock and topknot were tied last. The base of the topknot is tied with a cord made of tightly rolled cut paper (*motoyui*). The more strands bound around the base, the higher it rose, creating a more upright *mage*, which caused changes of hairstyle. To this topknot base (*ne*) all of the hair strands are brought and depend from it. Thus *ne* is the most important part in stabilizing the coiffure.

Professional hairdressers first appeared early in the Edo period to care for complex men's hair styles. In the late eighteenth century, women's hairdressing emerged as a separate profession, facilitating the appearance of more elaborate hairstyles. Hairdressers practiced in their own shops or visited private residences.

Mid-Edo period (end of 17th to first half of 18th century)

During this period, hair fashion dictated that side locks (*bin*) should not project out from the sides, but were instead to be pulled back against the head. The back hair was pulled down and then up, forming a downward-pointing fold of hair. Attention was paid to the chignon at the topknot for creating different shapes.

Hair ornaments were used, but only in moderation.

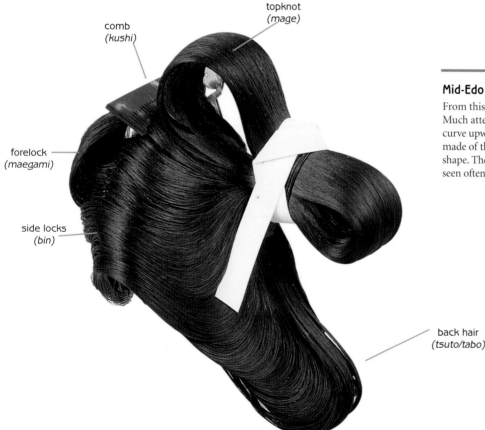

comb
(*kushi*)

topknot
(*mage*)

forelock
(*maegami*)

side locks
(*bin*)

back hair
(*tsuto/tabo*)

Mid-Edo to Late Edo period (second half of 18th century)

From this period on, hair dressing techniques developed remarkably. Much attention was paid to the back hair to make it long, and then to curve upward. In order to keep the puff away from the neck, a device made of thick black paper was used to pull the hair into a curved shape. These shapes, described as a "sea gull's tail" or "wagtail's tail," are seen often in prints of Suzuki Harunobu (1724–70).

Late Edo period (19th century)

Hairstyles became progressively more elaborate and complex. The side locks were rounded outward from the side of the head, and the back hair was pulled up into a short, roundish puff. The topknot was pulled to the back of the head, where elaborate ornamental combs and pins were inserted in it.

Karawa

*Hyōgo
Mage*

61

Young
man's
topknot

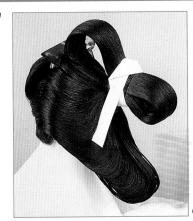
Shimada

63

Shimada
(Suzukii
Harunobu)

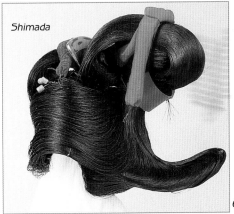
Shimada

66

*Dangling
kanzashi*
(Toyokuni I)

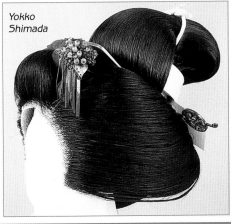
*Yokko
Shimada*

71

Hair Ornaments
Combs

During the Edo period, the custom of tying hair in elaborate shapes stimulated the use of fantastic hair ornaments. Before the Genroku (1688–1704) period, practical combs to comb hair were used as ornaments. They gradually became more ornamental. The major materials used for combs were boxwood (*tsuge*), which was lacquered with *maki-e*, and tortoise shell. The fashion of using two or three combs became prominent from 1716–1735. As the sidelocks were fashioned to extend farther and farther from the side of the head, more ornamental pins developed

72

Comb with Bush Clover and
  Telescopes
Maki-e on lacquered wood
Edo period, 19th century

This comb is decorated in *maki-e* with bush clover and two telescopes on the front; on the verso, the temple roofs and a pagoda are seen against mountains. The connection between the two scenes may be that these distant temples may be observed by the telescopes on the front side.

73

Comb with Sumiyoshi Shrine
Maki-e on lacquered wood
Inscription: *Jōka saku*
Edo period, 19th century

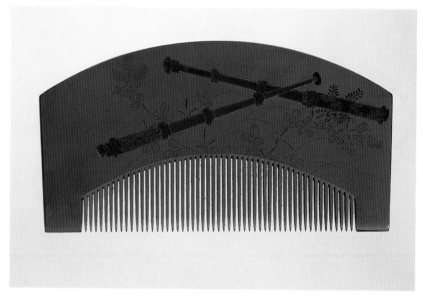

PI. 72

This comb is decorated on the front with a humped bridge and a *torii* gate near an ocean beach, and on the verso with a *torii* and a shrine building. These clues easily suggest the famous Sumiyoshi Shrine in Osaka, as do the characters from a poem, *Suminoe no,* on the front and *Kishi ni yume no kayoimichi* on the back, meaning "a dream path on a shore of Suminoe."

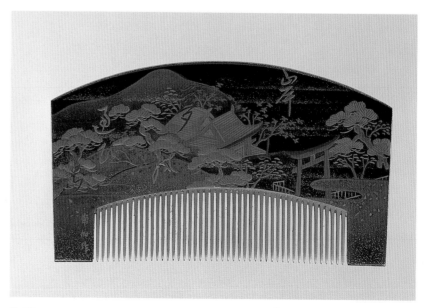

PI. 73

"Pony
tail"

Gosho Nage

62

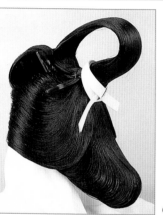

Katsuyama

65

Ryōwa

64

Katsuyama

Sakkō

67

Katsuyama

70

Ryōwa

69

Sakkō

68

61

Karawa (Chinese Ring)
17th-century style

The hair was tied in a knot on the top of the head. It became fashionable among kabuki actresses and professional women in the pleasure quarter.

62

Gosho Mage (Imperial Chignon)
17th-century style

This hairstyle was worn by ladies-in-waiting in the imperial court. Their long hair was twisted around and fastened by a stickpin (*kōgai*) on the back of the head. When the ladies were on duty, they removed the pin to let their hair down.

63

Shimada
Mid-Edo period, late 17th-first half of 18th century style

This style derived from the young man's topknot style. After the hair was tied at the top, the bundle of hair was brought forward and turned back toward the *ne*, making a loop. This hair loop was then tied together in the middle. Women of the pleasure quarter at the Shimada Station of the Tokaidō Road between Edo and Kyoto began to wear this hairstyle, hence its name. The *shimada* style became popular even among city women.

64

Ryōwa (Two Locks)
Late 17th century-first half of 18th century style

First worn by ladies-in-waiting in service to a daimyo, the *ryōwa* style became popular among middle-aged women of the merchant class. After the topknot was tied, the side locks were brought to the *ne* and were crossed and held in place by a stickpin (*kōgai*)

65

Katsuyama
Edo period, mid-17th century style

This hairstyle is said to have been started by a courtesan named Katsuyama. At the top back of the head, the hair was tied into a topknot and which was brought forward and then back to the base of the tie, forming a large loop. The loop was secured by a stickpin (*kōgai*) inserted from the sides. By the Genroku period (1688–1703) this style had spread to women in the general public.

66

Shimada
Edo period, second half of the 18th century style

The earlier, simpler *shimada* style developed into a fancy new style with a long, upward-curving, back-hair puff during the period from 1751 to 1772. It was very popular among daughters of merchants. Women with this hairdo were often depicted by Suzuki Harunobu (1724–1770) in his prints.

67

Sakkō
Second half of the 18th century style

This style resembles the *ryōwa* style, except that the topknot here turns up, while in the *ryōwa* style, it was turned down. Around the topknot, side locks are crossed around the stickpin (*kōgai*) which holds them in place.

68

Sakkō
19th century style

In this style, the long back hair was pulled out and up, making the neckline appear more rounded. The topknot was pulled up and made into a loop, which was crossed with side locks around a stickpin (*kōgai*). Other combs and pins were often used. This style was favored by young married merchant-class women in Kyoto.

69

Ryōwa (Two Locks)
19th century style

Merchant-class women in the Kyoto-Osaka region wore this hairstyle.

70

Katsuyama
19th century style

This hairstyle was worn by young maidens of seventeen to eighteen years old, from the well-to-do families in the Kyoto-Osaka region.

71

Yakko Shimada
19th century style

Daughters of samurai wore this style. Also called *taka shimada* (high *shimada*), the hair is tied higher in the back, making it look majestic. This *yakko shimada* hairdo was in the Kyoto style. Reflecting the late Edo period tendency, the back hair in this style curves up, making it shorter.

74

Comb with Scene of Pulling a Boat
Maki-e on lacquered wood
Edo period, 18th century

The front and the back of this comb are
decorated with a lyrical scene of men
pulling a boat in a river. The boat, with
passengers, is steered by a helmsman as
it is pulled with ropes by two men who
wear straw raincoats.

75

Comb with Ariwara no Narihira on
  His Way to the Eastern Provinces
Maki-e and gold inlay on lacquered wood
Edo period, 19th century

The theme of this comb is derived from
Ariwara no Narihira's journey to the
eastern provinces, taken from the *Tales
of Ise*. The figures of Narihira on
horseback and his attendant in relief
are covered in gold. On the back, Mt.
Fuji, in relief in gold, also suggests the
tale of the eastern provinces.

76

Comb with Hare's-foot Fern
Maki-e on lacquered tortoise shell
by Hara Yōyūsai (1768–1845)
Edo period, 19th century

Hara Yōyūsai, a *maki-e* craftsman, lived
in Kanda, Edo. He was a friend of Sakai
Hōitsu (1761–1828), the master painter
of the Rimpa school in Edo. Yōyūsai,
often decorated works designed by Hō
itsu. He especially excelled in applying
maki-e on small objects such as *inro*
and combs.
   This comb of tortoise shell is
decorated with hare's-foot ferns
(*Davallia bullata*) in *maki-e*. Dots of
red ladybugs add a lovely touch of
color.

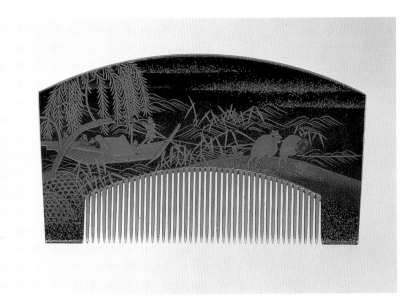

Pl. 74

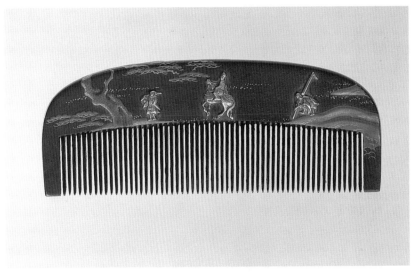

Pl. 75

Pl. 76

Kōgai

Kōgai at first were practical pins around which to roll the hair and to secure a bundle of hair on the head. They seem to have been in use by the 1680s. *Joyō kunmo zui* (Illustrated References for Women; 1687) shows a hairstyle with hair around the *kōgai* pin. A *kōgai* is a stick with identical shapes on both ends, and these ends are exposed when the sticks are inserted in the hair. In the late Edo period, *kōgai* became less practical and were used only to add a finishing touch to chignons or rolled hair. Such ornamental *kōgai* were made of two pieces of wood; a long stick with one end and one caplike piece on the other end. Some *kōgai* were made as a part of a set that included a comb. These sets were made with the same materials and decorated with similar motifs.

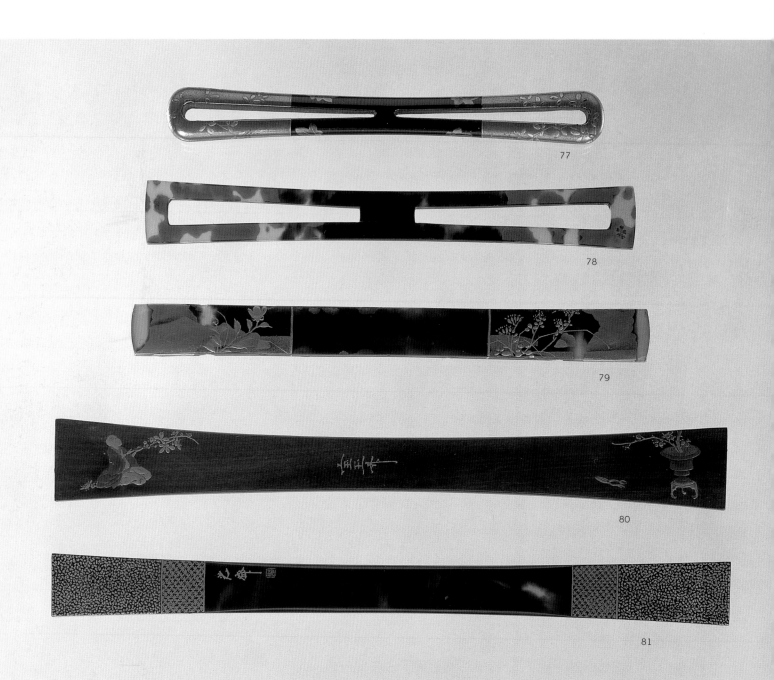

77

78

79

80

81

77

Kōgai with Bush Clover and
   Maple Leaves

Maki-e on lacquered wood

Edo period, 19th century

78

Kōgai with Clouds

Maki-e on tortoise shell

Edo period, 19th century

79

Kōgai with Autumn Plants

Maki-e on tortoiseshell

Edo period, 19th century

80

Kōgai with Flower Arrangement
   Theme

Maki-e on lacquered wood

by Hōgyoku

Edo period, 19th century

81

Kōgai with Hemp-Leaves

Maki-e and *kirikane* on tortoise shell

by Kosai

Edo period 19th century

Kirikane is thin gold foil cut into a
design and applied to the ground with
an adhesive.

82

Set of Comb, Short Pin, and *Kōgai*
with Mt. Fuji, Hawks, and Eggplants

Maki-e on lacquered wood

Edo period, 19th century

Each piece of this set is decorated with
the same motifs—Mount Fuji, two
hawks, and three eggplants. They are the
auspicious symbols that Japanese
wished to dream about on New Year's
night, in order for their wishes to come
true.

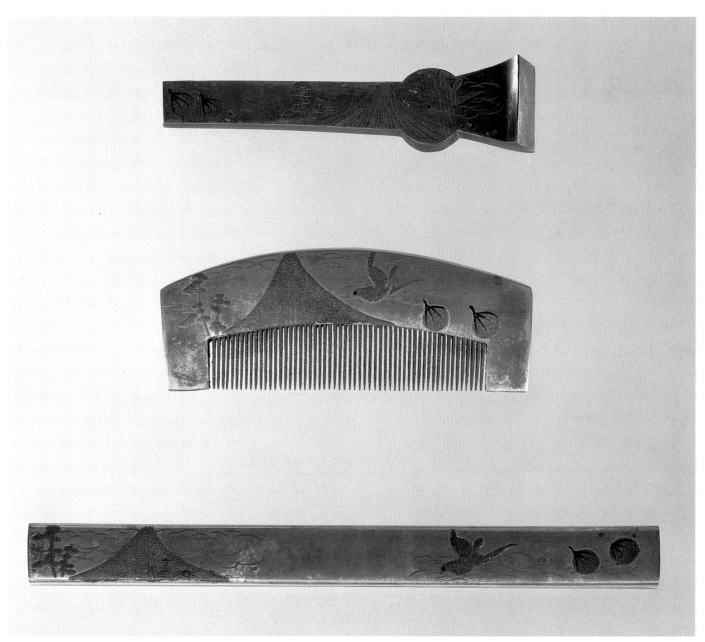

Pl. 82

Kanzashi

Kanzashi are ornamental hairpins for Japanese hairdos. Made of metal, *kanzashi* are shaped like pins with long prongs ending in a small spoon shape above the joined end. Ornaments, simple or elaborate, are attached just above where the prongs begin. *Kanzashi* came into use only after women's hair began to be tied, at first in modest styles, and very elaborately by the end of the nineteenth century. During the Genroku era (1688–1704), *kanzashi* were rarely used. During the early decades of the eighteenth century, however, simple *kanzashi* with flat, rounded ends, or ends in the shape of ginko leaves, began to appear. The spoon-shaped ends on *kanzashi* first appeared between 1716–1735 and gradually became more decorative.

In the nineteenth century, these pins were decorated with balls of precious materials such as tortoise shell, amber, jade, or witty decorations made of gold, silver, or corals.

83
Kanzashi with Shrimp
Metal and coral
Edo period, 19th century

84
Kanzashi with Clove
Metal and coral
Edo period, 19th century

85
Kanzashi with Bird on
 Branches
Metal and coral
Edo period, 19th century

86
Kanzashi with Basket and
 Various Treasures
Metal and coral
Edo period, 19th century

87
Kanzashi with Grapes and Vine
Metal and coral
Edo period, 19th century

88
Kanzashi with Tree Branch
 and Scissors
Metal and coral
Edo period, 19th century

88   87   86

89

Kanzashi with a Coral Ball
Metal and coral
Edo period, 19th century

90

Kanzashi with Amber Ball
Metal and amber
Edo period, 19th century

91

Kanzashi with *Tombodama* Ball
Metal and *tombodama*
Edo period, 19th century

Tombodama (lit. dragonfly ball) are lead glass beads that have other colored glasses inserted in the main body.

92

Kanzashi with *Tombodama* Ball
Metal and *tombodama*
Edo period, 19th century

93

Kanzashi with Shell
Metal and *maki-e* on shell
Edo period, 19th century

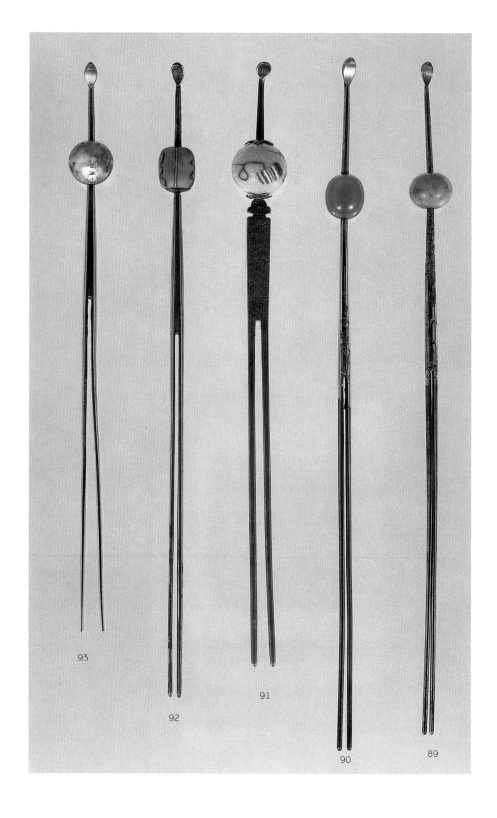

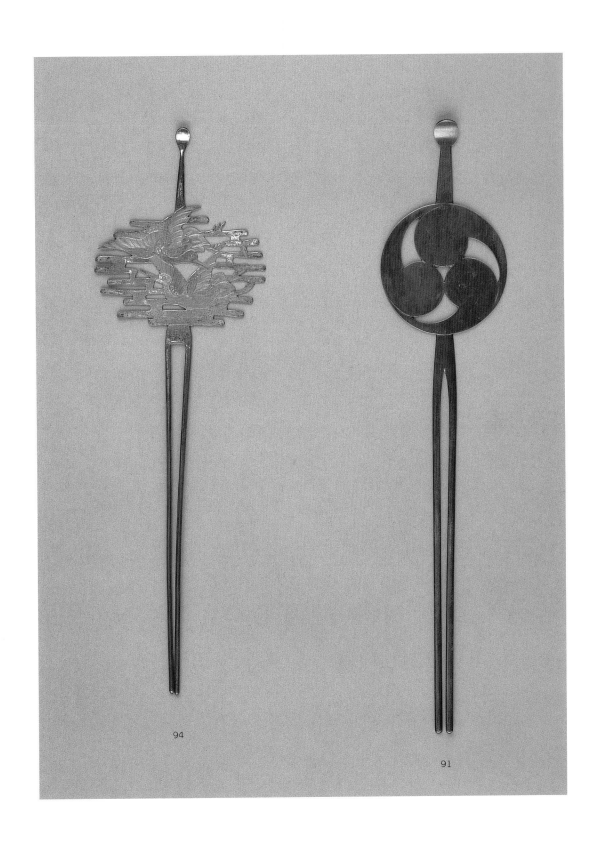

94

95

94

Kanzashi with Two Cranes
   Flying in Mist
Silver
Edo period, 19th century

This is a flat ornament type, called *hirauchi*.

95

Kanzashi with a Whirl of
   Three Commas
Metal
Edo period, 19th century

Dangling *Kanzashi*
(*bira bira kanzashi*)

Kanzashi with dangling ornaments of gold, silver, and coral were called *bira bira kanzashi*. They began to appear during the Gembun and Kampo eras (1736–1743), and in the Bunka Bunsei eras (1804–1830) they were in fashion. *Kanzashi* with lovely and delicate dangling objects were much favored by young maidens who looked beautiful in *furisode* (*kosode* with swinging sleeves), and by young newlywed women. For some reason, elaborate *kanzashi* dropped out of fashion and disappeared completely during the Bunkyu period (1861–1863).

96
Set of Two *Kanzashi* with Dangling
   Ornaments of Crane, Tortoise Shell,
   Pine, Bamboo, and Plum
Gold, silver, and coral
Edo period, 19th century

97
Set of Two *Kanzashi* with Dangling
   Ornaments of Peonies and Cherry
   Petals
Gold, silver, and coral
Edo period, 19th century

Pl. 96

Pl. 97

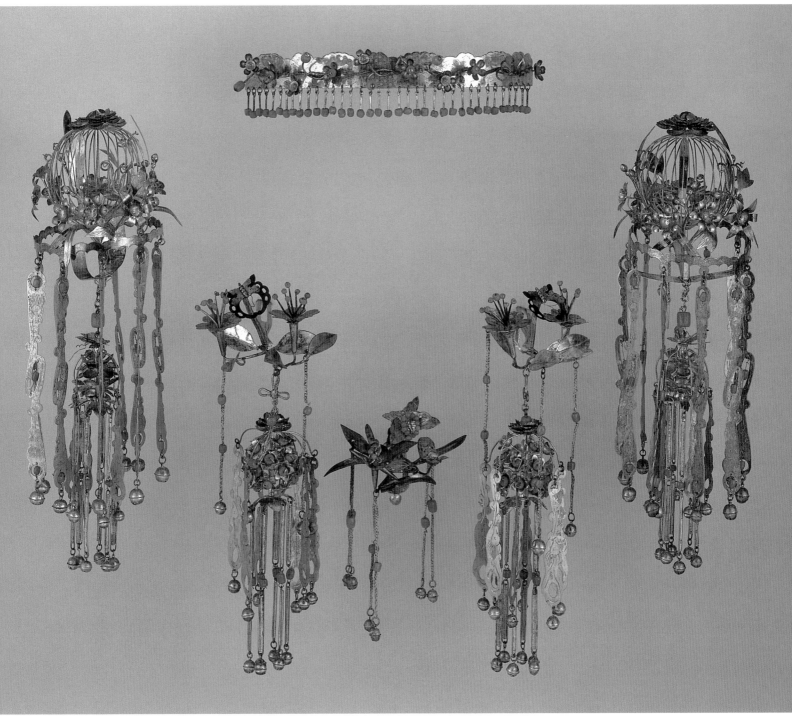

Pl. 98

98

Set of Six *Kanzashi* with Dangling
 Ornaments of Plum Blossoms, Bird
 Cages, Butterflies with *Kusudama*
 (ornamental perfumer), and
 Butterfly with *Omoto* (*Rhodea
 japonica*)
Gold, silver, and coral
Edo period, 19th century

PI. 99

99
Set of Five *Kanzashi* with Dangling
  Ornaments of Pine, Bamboo, and
  Plum, and Cranes and Tortoise Shell
Gold, silver, and coral
Edo period, 19th century

Pl. 100

100
Set of Five *Kanzashi* with Dangling
 Ornaments of Urashima Tarō Story
Gold, silver, and coral
Edo period, 19th century

Bibliography

100 Masterpieces from the Collection of the Suntry Museum of Art. Tokyo: Suntry Museum of Art, 1981.

Ban *Dainagon ekotoba* (Illustrated Handscroll of Ban Dainagon). Nihon emakimono zenshū, vol. IV. Tokyo: Kadokawa Shoten, 1965.

Burnham, Dorothy K. *Warp and Weft: A Textile Terminology*. Toronto: Royal Ontario Museum, 1964.

Collcutt, Martin, et al. *Cultural Atlas of Japan*. New York: Facts on File Publications, 1988.

Cooper, S. J. Michael, ed. *They Came to Japan; an Anthology of European Reports on Japan 1543-1640*. Berkeley: University of California Press, 1965.

Dalby, Liza. *Kimono: Fashioning Culture*. New Haven: Yale University Press, 1993.

Emakimono (Illustrated Handscrolls). Genshoku Nihon no bijutsu, vol. 8. Tokyo: Shogakukan, 1968.

Emery, Irene. *The Primary Structure of Fabrics: An Illustrated Classification*. Washington, D.C.: The Textile Museum, 1980.

Five Centuries of Japanese Kimono. Chicago: The Art Institute of Chicago, 1992.

Genji monogatari emaki to sanjūrokunin kashū (The Tale of Genji Handscroll and the Poems of the Thirty-Six Poets). Nihon bijutsu zenshū, vol. 9. Tokyo: Gakushū Kenkyūsha, 1977.

Haino, Akio. *Konrei dōgu* (Bridal Trousseaus). Nihon no bijutsu, no. 277. Tokyo, Shibundō, 1989.

Hashimoto, Sumiko. *Keppatsu to kamikazari* (Coiffure and Hair Ornaments). Nihon no bijutsu, no. 23. Tokyo: Shibundō 1968.

Hinonishi, Suketaka. *Fukushoku* (Costumes). Nihon no bijutsu, no. 26. Tokyo: Shibundō 1968.

Izutsu, Gafū. *Genshoku Nihon fukushoku-shi* (History of Japanese Costume in Color). Kyoto: Kōrinsha, 1982,

————. *Nihon josei fukushoku-shi* (History of Japanese Women's Costume). Kyoto: Kōrinsha, 1986.

Japan Textile Color Design Center. *Textile Designs of Japan*. 3 vols. Osaka: Japan Textile Color Design Center, 1960.

Kamiya, Reiko. *Kosode*. Nihon no bijutsu, no. 67, Tokyo: Shibundō, 1971.

Kawakami, Shigeki et al. *Yosooi: Nihon josei no bi* (Attire: the Beauty of Japanese Women). Fukuoka City: Fukuoka Municipal Museum, 1995.

————. *Kuge no fukushoku* (Imperial Robes). Nihon no bijutsu, no. 339. Tokyo: Shibundō, 1994.

Kasuga gongen genki-e (Illustrated Handscroll of Kasuga Gongen). Nihon emakimono zenshū, vol. XV. Tokyo: Kadokawa Shoten, 1963.

Kennedy, Alan. *Japanese Costume: History and Tradition*. Paris: Editions Adam Biro, 1990.

Kitamura, Tetsuo. *Yūzenzome* (Yuzen Dyeing). Nihon no bijutsu, no. 106. Tokyo: Shibundō, 1975.

Maruyama, Nobuhiko and Ishimura, Hayao. *Robes of elegance: Japanese Kimono of the 16th-20th Centuries*. Raleigh: North Carolina Museum, 1988

Miki, Fumio. *Haniwa: The Clay Sculpture of Proto-Historic Japan*. Tokyo: Charles E. Tuttle Co., 1960.

Minnich, Helen Benton. *Japanese Costume and the Makers of Its Elegant Tradition*. Tokyo: Charles E. Tuttle Co., 1963.

Nagasaki, Iwao. *Chōnin no fukushoku* (Costumes of Merchants). Nihon no bijutsu, no. 341. Tokyo: Shibundō, 1994.

Nishimura, Hyobu et al. *Tagasode: Whose Sleeves ... Kimono from the Kanebō Collection*. New York: Japan Society, 1976.

Rathbun, William Jay, ed. *Beyond the Tanabata Bridge: Traditional Japanese Textile*. Seattle: Seattle Art Museum, 1993.

Shaver, Ruth M. *Kabuki Costume*. Tokyo: Charles E. Tuttle Co., 1966.

Shōsō-in (Shoso-in Imperial Storage). Nihon bijutsu zenshū, vol. 5. Tokyo: Gakushu Kenkyūsha, 1978.

Stinchecum, Amanda Mayer. *Kosode: 16th-19th Century Textiles from the Nomura Collection*. New York: Japan Society and Kodansha International, 1984.

Takamatsu-zuka to Fujiwara-kyō; (Takamatsu-zuka Tomb and Fujiwara-kyō). Nihon bijutsu zenshū, v. 3. Tokyo: Gakushu Kenkyūsha. 1980.

Tamura, Shūji, ed. *Traditional Japanese Embroidery: Instructions for the Basic Techniques*. Togane City, Chiba: TEG (Kurenai-kai), n.d.

Textile Designs of Japan. 3 vols. Osaka: Japan Textile color Design Center, 1960.

Tsunoda, Ryūsaku and Goodrich, L. C. *Japan in the Chinese Dynastic Histories*. New York: Perkins Asiatic Monographs no. 2, 1951.

Wada, Yoshiko, et al. *Shibori: The Inventive Art of Japanese Shaped Resist Dyeing*. Tokyo: Kodansha International, 1983.

Yoshimura, Motoo. *Tamura corekushon: Kesho dogu to kamikazari* (Tamura Collection: Toiletry Articles and Hair ornaments). Kyoto: Shikosha, 1982.

Yoshioka, Tsuneo. *Nihon no Iro* (Colors of Japan) . Kyoto: Shikosha, 1983.

Appendix I

Traditional Kimono Colors

Photographs of dyed silk swatches.
Tsuneo Yoshioka, *Nihon no iro: Shokubutsu senryō no hanashi* (Colors of Japan: Story of Plant Dyestuffs), Shikōsha, 1983.
Photos: Shikōsha, Kyoto.

1. *kuchinashi* and *benibana* (gardenia, safflower) (combined color called *hanezu*)
2. *benibana* (*karakurenai*) safflower
3. *akane* (alum mordant) madder
4. *mutsuba akane* (alum mordant) six-leaf madder
5. *raku* (alum mordant) lac
6. *enji wata* (alum mordant) lac absorbed in cotton for transporting
7. *cochineal* (alum mordant) cochineal
8. *suō* (alum mordant) sappanwood
9. *murasaki kon* (alum mordant) gromwell root
10. *tade ai* and *benibana* (*futaai*) dyed with indigo from buckweat first, then safflower
11. *suō* (sulfuric acid and iron) sappanwood and mordants produce fake purple
12. *tade ai* (indigo from buckweat) see 10
13. *tade ai* dyed many times
14. *indo ai* (Indian indigo)
15. *kihada* (philodendron)
16. *ukon* (tumeric)
17. *kariyasu* (alum mordant) miscanthus
18. *enju* (alum mordant) larkspur
19. *yamamono* (evergreen tree)
20. *saffron* (saffron)
21. *tade-ai* and *kihada* (indigo and philodendron)
22. *tade-ai* and *kariyasu* (indigo and miscanthus)
23. *asen* (Japanese cutch)
24. *cutch* (cutch)
25. *tsurobami* (beech)
26. *kurumi* (walnut)
27. *zakuro* (pomegranate)
28. *chōji* (clove)
29. *ume* (plum)
30. *gobaishi* (gallnut)
31. *binroju* ((beetlenut)
32. *logwood* (logwood)

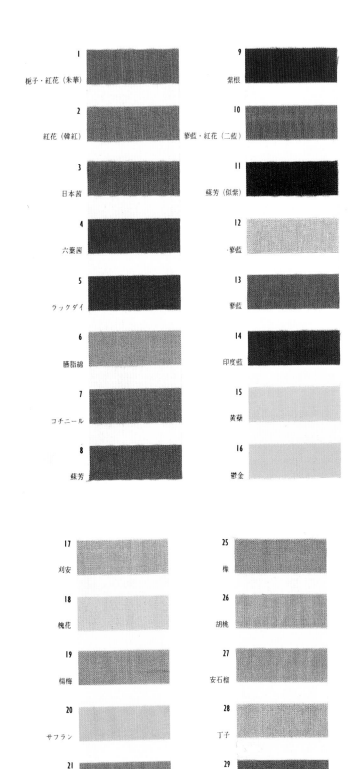

1 梔子・紅花（朱華）	9 紫根		
2 紅花（韓紅）	10 蓼藍・紅花（二藍）		
3 日本茜	11 蘇芳（似紫）		
4 六葉茜	12 ·蓼藍		
5 ラックダイ	13 蓼藍		
6 臙脂綿	14 印度藍		
7 コチニール	15 黄蘗		
8 蘇芳	16 鬱金		
17 刈安	25 橡		
18 槐花	26 胡桃		
19 楊梅	27 安石榴		
20 サフラン	28 丁子		
21 蓼藍・黄蘗	29 梅		
22 蓼藍・刈安	30 五倍子		
23 阿仙	31 檳榔樹		
24 カッチ	32 ログウッド		

Appendix II

Chronology

JŌMON PERIOD	ca.12,000–250 BC
YAYOI PERIOD	ca. 250 BC–AD 250
KOFUN PERIOD	250–552
ASUKA PERIOD	552–710
NARA PERIOD	710–794
HEIAN PERIOD	794–1185
KAMAKURA PERIOD	1185–1333
NANBOKUCHŌ PERIOD	1333–1392
MUROMACHI PERIOD	1392–1573
MOMOYAMA PERIOD	1573–1615
Tenshō era	1573–1592
Keichō era	1596–1614
EDO PERIOD	1615–1868
EARLY EDO	1615–1688
Genna era	1615–1624
Kanei era	1624–1644
Kanbun era	1661–1673
MID-EDO	1688–1789
Genroku era	1688–1704
Meiwa era	1764–1772
LATE EDO	1789–1868
Bunka era	1804–1818
Bunsei era	1818–1830
MEIJI PERIOD	1868–1912
TAISHŌ PERIOD	1912–1926
SHŌWA PERIOD	1926–1989
HEISEI	1989–

Index